TAKING THE QUANTUM LEAP

PROPHETESS HEATHER SCANTLEBURY

Ordering Information:

Prime Seven Media
518 Landmann St.
Tomah City, WI 54660

Printed in the United States of America

Table of Contents

Foreword

*W*e live in a rapidly changing world where understanding and adapting are crucial. As a minister of the gospel, I am deeply concerned about how many people live their lives, relying on outdated or ineffective systems yet expecting different results. Consistently using flawed methods will only yield the same disappointing outcomes.

Many Christians struggle to fully understand God's system for achieving results, overlooking the principles and laws that enable His system to respond favorably. Often, churchgoers focus solely on receiving blessings, neglecting the foundational understanding of their divine purpose. While it is right to expect and hope for breakthroughs, we must first know who we are, why God has chosen us, and focus on fulfilling our purpose, allowing rewards to follow.

Unrealistic expectations without understanding our role often lead to frustration and disillusionment with God. To avoid this, every individual must actively participate in shaping their life. God intervenes when divine assistance is needed, but our consistent effort is vital.

This book, *Taking the Quantum Leap*, is written to guide you in aligning your life with God's purpose, enabling you to live your best life now. It's not about past struggles or emotions but about taking actionable steps to transform every aspect of your life. With ability, wisdom, and divine power, you can recover and fulfill the life God destined for you.

I urge you to embark on this new chapter of living life on God's terms. With divine guidance and supernatural support, your best life is within reach. Answer the call—it's time to begin.

CHAPTER 1

Taking the Quantum Leap.

Most people create goals and have dreams for their lives so that they can begin to move in the direction of making their lives greater, much more fulfilling and satisfying. They have an inherent understanding and belief that life is supposed to be lived and lived well. They want to achieve more from where they are, and therefore they set out on a journey seeking such a life with the expectation and confidence that it can and will happen.

They understand that in pursuing such a dream, to make it a reality, there are certain criteria required to keep them on the journey and to meet whatever challenges and obstacles that will present themselves whether to hinder, slow them down or even divert and make them think twice to change their minds.

Every person can have their dream life and live it. The opportunities, tools and necessary information are all available to assist in the pursuit of such, however even though this is true and can be achieved it must be realized that not everyone will become very persuaded and convicted enough to make this a reality in their lives.

Sometimes many people are not very certain or sure as to what they really want to achieve and how they want the outcome of their lives to be. Even when given a picture of how their lives can be and with the aid of God how He wants our lives to be and what is His plan for us.

I have met so many people who, when talking with them, make you believe that they are very certain about themselves. They have these very necessary areas and segments of their lives covered then to realize they are moving in a direction completely opposite to what they are saying and where they plan to go.

We must become very watchful of our lives, our dreams and goals and make the necessary adjustments, changes and transitions to reach the destination we are destined to reach. Even if at the beginning stages of the journey we were not totally convinced and convicted of the outcome.

Getting on the journey will make a whole lot of difference in our thinking and perception of life and how it is in comparison to how we can make it.

Let's take the journey to ... Taking the Quantum Leap!!!!

What is the Quantum Leap?

To make an abrupt transition from one place to greater one.

A sudden and Significant Change.

To Advance or to Increase.

To experience life in another dimension will demand change. Depending on the dimension, the change must become similar and of the same quality. Many people are desirous of fame and a greater way of living, they want to know and experience life at the best level and there is nothing wrong with such desires and goals.

However, when the mind has not been renewed and adjusted to live at such a level, or it does not understand that there are required changes for such levels, the appreciation and meshing can become very difficult and the success at that level can dwindle just as quickly as it is achieved.

Experiences without change are meaningless and will never be appreciated or cherished.

It can be dangerous to live on a level that you have not made any preparations for or significant changes. **Hence the Quantum Leap is necessary.**

In pursuing a better life and adapting to such, then it must be very evident that change must become very necessary and vital, not only in the achieving but also in the maintaining.

Therefore, The Quantum Leap is something that is sudden and significant happening to me for the better that gives me **A Total Ongoing Life Changing Experience.**

Why the Quantum Leap now in your life?

The Age we are living in is asking and demanding such.

To achieve the best life can offer.

To live the best way and see your dreams become a reality.

To know and experience the ease in all levels of life.

Start confessing the above, tell yourself these are what you deserve and give yourself permission to go after them.

Now is the time for every individual to renew their minds and tailor them in the direction of being Successful and having phenomenal Experiences in Life that will make life interesting and exciting, hence creating a Passion for life.

Every person must have **Productivity and Increasing on their minds. Life was not given to be wasted or abused, life has been given to be Maximized** at every level and dimension.

The Age *we are living in is asking and demanding such.*

What do we mean by the age we are living at?

Age is defined as a set period of time destined to bring the full maturity and state of all things to a place of completion where they are at their highest quality and quantity and are ready and fit for use.

It is also a set or allotted time given to human life, usually marked by a certain stage or degree of mental or physical development and involving greater and higher responsibilities and capacities to excel over and above.

Now is that set time and period for us to begin to see extraordinary things begin to unfold and manifest where we are, for our families and loved ones. It is also the period or set time designed by God our heavenly Father for all forms and all types of Perfect Manifestations to come to the body of Christ.

Now at this point of history, many people are moving from just being millionaires to billionaires and the rapidity of such has become mind blowing and troubling to many, but that is what usually happens when the full ripeness of an age has come.

Therefore, every individual who desires such levels of living and experiences must understand that there is a quality and level of change needed to trigger the actual results expected.

Even though there are many chaotic things happening in our region and around the world, we must see these as signs calling to us for change and change at every level and dimension.

In the book of Hebrews, Chapter 1: 10 – 12 it reads:

*And (further) You Lord did lay **the foundation of the earth in the beginning, and the heavens** are the works of Your hands.*

*They will perish, but You remain and continue permanently, **they will all grow old and wear out like a garment.***

*Like a mantle (thrown about one's self) **You will roll them up and they will be changed and replaced by others,** but You remain the same, and Your years will never end or come to failure.* **Hebrews 1:10-12 Amplified Version**

The world we knew years ago and even in 2016 has changed so much. The one we currently live in has called and is still calling for greater change and we must understand the language to make the types of changes it demands, so that it can exist and function by its intended purpose. That familiar world no longer exists, and we must begin to understand and embrace such.

Even though there is much misunderstanding concerning what is happening, the interpretation even from men and women of the Kingdom is giving too many mixed messages, states of confusion and it is very evident that it is not business as usual anymore. Significant changes are taking place and will continue to take place whether we are prepared and ready for the changes that are coming.

It is declared here in the scripture given above, that even the very foundations of both earth and heaven will become old and worn and will be replaced. How much more than must we be realizing that there are certain appointed times that demand the highest levels of change to ensure that we become the very highest versions of ourselves?

We must constantly be aware of the times we are in so that we can take the appropriate action. When we live oblivious to the language of the age, much can creep up upon us and bring results that we in many cases don't need and want.

Some of the greatest areas that change does not seemingly get to fully penetrate are within the Mindset, Consciousness and Hearts of people. When change gets to perform its entire operation as it is designed to do, then the exchange will take place to bring impact so that God's reality can come into place.

Even many who believe and say they have a tremendous, good working mindset, and consciousness, show that their levels of operation are so Obscured that it makes what they are saying seem so meaningless and the level of impact that they can bring is not coming.

Whenever the mindset and consciousness are constantly renewed and developed, a greater level of operation will and must come forth to bring into effect the now purpose and will of God. We need to see the will of God in a greater dimension in effect in our lives, families, homes and nation.

You must believe and embrace with everything in you that the age we are in that's being designed by God our Father is here, ready and set to give you some supernatural defining moments in your life that will not only make you happy but will always change your views and purposes towards life and how destiny is designed to unfold for every person.

Anything that refuses to change will die.

Personal Reasons for Taking The Quantum Leap.

God is very interested in you personally achieving the best in life and out of life. He is desirous of your life becoming great, fulfilling and rewarding.

It's your time to experience Supernatural Defining Moments from the Divine Higher and Greater realm. This is how your life is supposed to be.

He has made all the provisions you need, supplied all the help and assistance that will take you where He has planned for you and the destination He has for you to arrive at. **You Are Not Alone in This.**

The higher and greater one becomes in knowledge, wisdom, growth and development in all areas of life, the higher and greater opportunities become available. Here is where the circle of people increases and changes. Without doubt so will the Favor, Grace Anointing, your personal creativity, abilities and capabilities will begin to function greater.

Here in the Scripture, we read,

"THE Sons of the prophets said to Elisha, Look now, the place where we live before you **is too small for us.**

Let us go to the Jordan, and each man get there a [house] beam; and let us make us a place there where we may dwell. And he answered, Go.

One said, Be pleased to go with your servants. He answered, I will go."

2 Kings 6:1-3 Amplified Version.

From biblical insight of the place Jordan, let's see the Jordan as the place of many Activities.

Something is always happening at Jordan in season and even out of season. There is the time of great overflowing. So much constant activity happening at the Jordan. This is how our lives have been designed By God: something is always happening. Activity in our lives must not be restricted by seasons.

You must recognize when your life has become so cramped with people or in doing so much that the results level is diminished where there is little or no significant progress, when in your heart you know things should be greater and better and things should be happening.

Things can and will stop working when there is no growth and the consciousness is no longer being developed to receive greater realities to assist your life to the next level.

You should know when it is time to make critical decisions and moves that can and will bring change to your life in an extraordinary way. When there is much hesitation and the inability to act when the opportunity arises, very often the moment and the atmosphere to make things happen moves on until it finds the ready person who will take a position and make the decision to act for the results that are being offered.

These guys from the above scripture knew when the time was ripe for making the decision to have the change they needed. They were completely frustrated at being uncomfortable and barely accepting the norm. They wanted better and they believed that they were able together to have better, hence they made the decision and followed through on it.

You must be alert when your heart says to the mind, I'm uncomfortable and the mind says it's ok just bear it we can make out with this. It is not right to be uncomfortable and pretend it's okay when you can go to another place and experience the comfort that will bring out the best in you.

Personal understanding and awareness become very active when the Quantum Leap has been done. Let's become very sure that I our personal life the quantum leap is what we need right now.

Every person really wants to achieve big in life and they want to see their hopes and dreams become a reality. Honestly, we all want the best that life offers, therefore, its time to take action.

It's Time to make up your mind to Achieve the Best God offers and Live well at all Levels.

Living life on God's terms offers everyone the best Life ever. It is very important to know what terms God is offering us and make the adjustment so that we can really begin to live well, be well and do well.

This is a tough statement, but it is a very necessary and factual one that must guard your life.

Based on the correct view you have of God and the world; the God you embrace you will see him work for you. If you have the wrong view of a thing, it can work as effectively as it is designed to for you and even in your life.

Personally, many people have the wrong concept and view of God and the world, so they never really get to understand themselves, the world we are in, the world that God loves and then God himself.

Many just co-exist with how things are, and they accept them as a way of life just hoping and wishing that one-day things may eventually change, maybe a fairy god mother or father will show up.

The Scripture here says:

*For I know **the thoughts and plans** I have for you, says the Lord, Thoughts and plans for welfare and peace and not for evil, to give you hope in your outcome.* **Jeremiah 29: 11 Amplified Version**

I know what I am doing, I have it all planned out – plans to take care of you, not to abandon you, plans to give you the future you hope for. **Jeremiah 29: 11 Message Version**

Can you imagine that God has been and is thinking about you? Look at the level of thinking He has in His mind concerning you and what is the outcome of the thoughts He is thinking.

Know that God is taking the time to have the correct ideas and opinion produced by His process of thinking. He's taking the time to carefully give us His full attention so that whatever comes into His mind is of Superior quality. We obviously had to have His full attention so that when He reviews himself and considers us, in His mind the only formed picture and view of us is that he really wanted to see abilities and attributes of Himself in us manifested.

He so masterfully controlled His thinking that it brought out the best thoughts ever about us. Very often it is very difficult to control our thinking furthermore to become skilled at our creation from the mind and then to reality.

Most people have not really understood the concept of God being the greatest father and the relationship and obligation of a father to his children and his children to their father.

Sometimes when speaking with many individuals both male and female, they never knew what it is to have a father in their lives. For those who did have a father most times the relationship has not grown as it needs to, or it has not been established the way it needs to. Then there are those who knew a father's love and care and it has taught them well how to relate to their father and how to maintain the relationship that will work for them all the time.

Whether we go to church or not there must be the perfect view and perception of God that He is a loving Father who is perfect in all His ways. This perfection is equipped with all the knowledge, wisdom and characteristics that are required for the best life and will enable you to become great, unstoppable and having that life.

The message version has so carefully and masterfully structured this verse, for us to see a Loving Father who already planned the outcome of life for His children. Here it is,

I know what I am doing, I have it all planned out – plans to take care of you, not to abandon you, plans to give you the future you hope for.

Jeremiah 29: 11 Message Version

In examining this verse carefully, you can imagine and begin to the see how great and skilled is the experience the Father is speaking from, the confidence He has, to give us the assurance that we can leave it all in his hands and be assured that if we followed the design and do our part then we will have the life that is successful and ever so fulfilling.

He also allows us to know and understand, it is possible to think just like Him and imagine at the highest level of consciousness the type of life we can have as (His) children of the King and then to accept his reality as our very own.

The message from Him to us is very loud and clear, there is no need to worry, be frustrated, think negatively or be stressed out and believe that your life will not work out. What we must be concerned about here is that we become so seriously committed to the Father's plan and ideals for our lives that we begin to work with Him to make His plans become a reality.

So many people have been longing and looking for someone with the qualities, who is deemed as the right person to come into their lives, one who will look out for their wellbeing and ensure they have the desired outcome in life. Well, here is the Father of all fathers letting us know, He is the One, this is really His purpose in life for us and if we accept His plan for how our lives will eventually become.

Very often it may seem difficult to know or have clarity in making the moves to begin the process to get on the path, but it don't have to be that difficult. If you have seriously decided to do it, personally allow your mind and being permission to believe. Accept this plan offered and the fact beyond any doubt that you are deserving and worthy of a better life.

Tell yourself that your life can become a thousand times better no matter where it is. Finally make plans for change. In some cases, you may have to shift some people currently in your life for a season and ask the Lord to bring the correct people in your life from this point onward. People who are interested in where you need to go and will assist you in getting there.

Assistance does not always come in the form of money, even though you will need money, but there is some vital information (tools, knowledge, strategies, concepts, discipline, adapting, and the list goes on) that's very necessary to assist you on how to structure your life. Also, how to easily move from where you are, and the ongoing support and encouragement to keep you on track and to keep your goals alive and fresh.

I declare for all you my readers that God begins to create avenues to new open doors in your lives, that you will be in the right place at the right time to meet the right people and today begins a new and greater chapter in your lives.

Dreams, goals and desires will be fulfilled and the energy and passion level about life rises to the level needed to make unusual, good things happen for you.

Agree with me and see your new life unfold and transform supernaturally. All the people, tools, information, money and facilities will become available to you supernaturally that you will begin to be more conscious of God and His Design and Purpose for you, now!! than you have ever been in your lifetime.

Make this your daily affirmation. I am deserving of the best life, I believe with all of me that this is how my life has been designed to be, to have all the good and perfect things in motion.

I see my life becoming great and unending, filled with all the good things that life should offer that will enhance my life and make me happier than I have ever been.

Therefore, I receive only the good and the perfect and I renounce anything that will cause me distress, worry or frustration. From today, I will constantly renew my mind and my consciousness will be upgraded, and I will now take action in setting my sub consciousness on assignment to bring only the good and perfect operation in my life.

CHAPTER 2

Capturing your own attention:

It's time to Capture Your own attention.

Many times, we assist people, help them to their next dimension and level of living and forget ourselves, our own personal needs, potential and abilities. We often tell ourselves we will eventually have time for ourselves, not realizing that time is not waiting on or for us.

Unnoticed, time has swiftly passed and there were so many opportunities with the next level of living for us that we missed. Even though we have assisted people to their next level, when we need assistance those same people are not there for us and they have dwindled from their place and have not even secured their place to the next level.

It seems that we must be constantly there for them and leave ourselves undone. Even if you consider making such a decision you must put careful thought and study to it before taking such a position as these same individuals can become a problem in your life. Hence it is time to capture yourself. Let the Focus be on you now!

First, you must forget and stop focusing and paying too much attention to all the time that has been wasted, what you could have done and didn't do, where you could have been and currently not there. It is not the season to spend time on wasted time, regrets and unfulfilled dreams and desires.

Now that you are here at this critical juncture of your life, be very certain of what you really want to do. It is very important that you are certain of what you want to do and where you can visualize yourself going. Then, begin to create a new plan, one that you will be serious enough to commit to and make plans to act to secure your successful present and future.

While in pursuit of your dreams, desires and goals I'm sure you will find another you that is very unknown and surprising to you and a reality of how your life is designed to be. It is vital and necessary to find out that reality of who you really are and what has been said about you. There is more to you than what you currently see, know and believe. Get on the journey to finding a greater you that is so **Gifted Beyond Measure**.

In the book of Psalms chapter 40: verses 7-8 Amplified Version

Then said I, Behold I come; in the volume of the book, it is written of me, I delight to do Your Will O my God, Yes, Your Law is written within my heart. **Psalms 40:7-8 Amplified Version**

Also in Hebrews Chapter 10: verse 7 **Amplified Version**

Then I said, Behold, here I am coming to do Your Will O God – (to fulfil) what is written of me in the volume of the Book. **– Hebrews 10:7 Amplified Version**

If we carefully examine these two scriptures, we will begin to realize that even Jesus, being the Son of God would have understood His father's plan yet He (Jesus) took the time to search the volume of the book to find out what was written about him.

He did this so that it would be clear to all that even though, He being the son of God, wanted to make it very clear about the plan of the father where his life and existence were concerned. He checked out what was the plan, submitted to it and then got busy making it a reality.

He makes it absolutely clear he's coming to fulfil what is in writing about Him. To do this, it would mean that Jesus took the time to find out all that has been said about Him, maybe ponder on them for some time to allow his mind to accept those things as His own reality, then focus on himself to the point of submitting to this reality that He can position and adjust himself to take on such a task.

He would then renew his mind so much to become so mentally strong that no matter how great the job was, what it consists of, he must do what he came here to do.

This level of positioning will take mental strength, focus and adhering to the structure designed to make all of this happen exactly how it is designed to take place.

Very often most people become skilled at being able to capture the attention of others. They seem to have employed much thought and study in this activity because they have studied their plan and have already envisioned the outcome. Therefore, when the opportunity presents itself

PROPHETESS HEATHER SCANTLEBURY

for them there is not much to do because they have become so skilled in making it happen.

It is now time to employ that same time, energy and focus on yourself to make some urgent evaluations and make the critical changes that are necessary for things to begin to move in your life and to have the desired outcome.

Here are a few important reasons why it is time to capture your own attention.

- To find all your untapped gifts, talents and abilities. Just to know how gifted You are.

- To find higher and greater versions of yourself.

- To evaluate oneself to see whether you have made significant change for the times and seasons that are here.

- To know whether you are relevant and have grown in understanding, knowledge and maturity to handle any challenge that may come into your life.

- To make improvements where needed.

- To constantly have timely encounters predetermined and scheduled by the Divine Realm.

- To review your life, to be happy and excited with the change you have made with you and what you are molding yourself to be.

Therefore, let's take the journey in exploring yourself.

20

Exploring You from the inside out.

Hidden realities:

Over the years, with much experience in having the opportunity to talk and deal with people, it is amazing the things you will learn about them and from them.

Most people have mastered the ability to use charisma to charm people, get their attention and even draw people into the web they so cleverly weaved over the years, but they have never worked enough on themselves to reproduce a well-rounded and balanced individual and at the same time propel others grow and mature.

They are of the perception and belief that they are so smart they can evade anything or anyone and live double lives. They produce a set of rules and values for others to live by while they produce another set to live their lives by.

They know what is right and wrong when it comes to another person's activity while they do exactly what they criticize and deem inappropriate.

In studying such individuals, it Is very clear how warped the mind is and how often the individual lives in an unconscious state of reality or rather their reality is so far from the proven and accepted reality. This can become very frightening, because these individuals have exposed themselves to any type and level of activity that will make you wonder whether there is any God consciousness at work within them.

You must never let your mind go that far below the graph or bar of right and wrong. The key to ensuring this never happens is to guard your mind and constantly renew it. The control over the mind is in your hands and you must be at work twenty-four seven to keep the mind under control and guarded from such activity and behavior.

I challenge you to take a little test. Are you like that?

Say one thing and then do exactly what you say you will never find yourself caught in?

Do you operate by having double standards and feel that it is alright to be like that? Now is the time to quit this activity in your life, things are no longer the same and as time changes, change expects everyone to be involved with it.

People often make the statement, *"well no one is perfect, every person has faults, show me a man who has no faults and I'll show you a dead person."*

This is true to some degree; however, we must be willing to work profusely to eliminate bad practices that will create faults and failure in our lives and set our minds in the direction of creating the highest and greatest version of oneself in all areas of life.

Exploring our lives to see whether over the years our lifestyle has become so damaging to our Character and the integrity of who we are and what we profess to be.

It must be noted very carefully that your character can make room for you or collapse every catwalk you are destined to walk.

I urge you, in all that you do and seek in life, to ensure that you choose to have an astounding and untarnished character. Be very careful of the lifestyle you have practiced over the years, what you practice after such length of time, you will master and become very skilled at.

When people become aware of your lifestyle even though they may not say anything to you they will eventually lose respect and honor for you, because your way of life has become a blocker to them and their personal expectations of and from you are dashed into pieces.

It is not very hard for people to know whether you are shady or not, and it does not even matter how talented you are. People expect that rule makers live by the same rules they make, or they even have greater and higher rules for themselves.

Sometimes the shady lifestyle can be hidden by charisma, talents and gifts, for a season and very often the season can go on for years, but it must be very clear that time and seasons will end to begin another dimension of time, seasons and events. When the season is over, the shade(s) will be removed and other people will get to see who you really are, the rules and standards you live by will determine whether they can continue to hold you in the esteem they have done over the years.

Going on this journey will also open your eyes to let you see how this practiced lifestyle has diminished the level of success, fame and prosperity you were designed to have. It should bring you to the realization of how you have been delayed from reaching your true potential and become the individual that has the abilities, talents, gifts and knowledge to be great.

This lifestyle will eventually kill greatness, even if certain levels of greatness is achieved. Don't kill or diminish the huge Greatness that is on the inside of you.

The journey to exploring you is to ensure that all the potential blockers and killers that you have constructed in your life over the years are demolished to make you ready for success and the great lasting life.

Hidden realities:

As we continue the journey to exploring yourself, let's find out what else has been hidden that needs to surface now in your life.

These untapped talents and gifts that are urgently asking for activation and release to give you the advantage.

Here in the book of Genesis chapter 12: verses 1-3, we read,

1 NOW [in Haran] the Lord said to Abram, Go, for yourself **[for your own advantage]** away from your country, from your relatives and your father's house, to the land that I will show you. [Heb. 11:8-10.]

2 And I will make of you a great nation, and I will bless you [with abundant increase of favours] and make your name famous and distinguished, and you will be a blessing [dispensing good to others].

3 And I will bless those who bless you [who confer prosperity or happiness upon you] and curse him who curses or uses insolent language toward you; **in you will all the families and kindred of the earth be blessed [and by you they will bless themselves].** [Gal. 3:8.] **Genesis 12 Verses 1-3 Amplified Version.**

Now this scripture first dealt with Abraham and how God Spoke to him and made a request of him to which he obeyed but look at what was coming behind the obedience. As we know Abraham obeyed God and got to live an extraordinary life that He became an icon of biblical history and is still mentioned and referred to even in our time.

However, as you examined verse three (3) carefully not only was God speaking to and about Abraham, but we were included in this awesome and phenomenal word of blessing. Yes, we were included, *"In you (Abraham) will all the families and kindred of the earth be blessed [and by you they will bless themselves]."*

This is so powerful, and mind provoking to even imagine and consider that all that time when God showed up to talk with Abraham he was also thinking of you and your family. To solidify this let's look at another scripture to cement this aspect of fact that we so often miss and never get to use for our advantage.

Galatians Chapter 3: verse 8 and 9.

8 *And the Scripture, foreseeing that God would justify (declare righteous, put in right standing with Himself)* **the Gentiles in** *consequence of faith, proclaimed the Gospel [foretelling the glad tidings of a Saviour long beforehand] to Abraham in the promise, saying,* **in you shall all the nations [of the earth] be blessed.** *[Gen. 12:3.]*

9 *So then, those who are people of faith are blessed and made happy and favoured by God [as partners in fellowship] with the believing and trusting Abraham.*

Galatians 3:8-9 Amplified Version.

This should cancel every doubt in you that you would believe, accept this as your designed way of life by the father and check carefully on the inside to see what gifts have been deposited in you to work on this prophecy to make this a reality in your life and that of your family.

Your thinking should either change or be accelerated to another dimension to see how it is supposed to be for All families in the earth. Very often the lack of knowing certain truths and embracing them to make them your very own so that they can find the right mechanism on the inside to produce the inevitable can be lost.

The goals and desires are so low because the believing in many cases has not grown, increased or adjusted to accept higher things. Often, the food needed to nurture it and ensure that the quality and speed needed to bring maturity have not been realized.

It is important that you believe the word of God. I have met so many people who are very skeptical and even voice words like I don't believe in God. But one thing is very sure and real, this plan of action, where all of this is concerned was done before any of us came to the earth realm, and proves with all clarity that God believes in all of us.

This act states very clearly **God (He) believed in You before you got to the earth realm then and will believe in you even more now** and will keep doing His part until we finally accept His plan and have this active in our lives.

What you must do now is to believe in You.

As we consider His plan and design that prompts us to become people of faith, He blesses us, makes us happy and ensures that we are favored by Him and others.

This favor will work for us and allow us to realize that on the inside there is His investment that will work for us and in many cases allow us to experience Greatness and live lives of greatness. Favor can show up for us in many different forms and it is very important to have God's favor on our lives and working.

Always embrace the mindset that you are earmarked for greatness and to live the life of greatness.

Getting rid of slowness to act, in critical situations.

Now we are on the path of paying serious attention to ourselves and making the moves that are very necessary to take the Quantum Leap, we want to look at all the areas that can hinder our progress.

We must never let ourselves be so trapped by external conditions and situations that stop us from taking the action needed to improve our lives no matter what.

There are too many people who have hesitated so much when they are faced with critical decision making and have lost some awesome life changing opportunities. That must no longer happen to you no matter how great the challenge.

God is the God of productivity and He loves it, when His children understand this concept of Himself and how they (His children) are supposed to be and have things constantly moving in their lives. He (God) dislikes unproductivity.

I was reading the below quote and it really gave me much to think about and I realized that there is so much hidden truth in it if you can view this through the right eyes.

Here is the quote,

"We generate fears while we sit. We overcome them by action. Fear is nature's way of warning us to get busy." ~ Dr. Henry Link

Many people will tell you of all the dreams they had, but never go to live them just because of fear. They never had the ability to break through their barriers of fears to achieve their dreams and desires. This is due to having the wrong understanding and message of how fear is generated and how seriously it can affect individuals

Here Dr. Henry Link shows us that while we do nothing or become slow to act, fear is generated. Not acting gives our minds the leverage to become very filled and crowded with doubt and doubt will eventually breed fear.

When individuals are too at ease, unproductive, fear is generated. It is very clear that unnoticed there is the creating, producing and bringing into existence fear that will eventually wok against us.

The Biblical teaching on fear is that fear is a spirit and we were never given such a spirit

2 Timothy Chapter 1: verse 7

For God did not give us a spirit of timidity (of cowardice of craven and cringing and fawning fear) but He has given us a spirit of power and of love and of calm and well-balanced mind and discipline and self -control. 2 Timothy 1:7 Amplified Version

Wow this is awesome! God did not give us this spirit of fear, but it has bee allowed to do a masterfully job in stopping many from achieving their dreams and to stop many from running vigorously towards the finishing line.

The amazing things that caught my attention were these attributes mentioned that have been given to ensure that fear never fills spaces in our lives. It allows us to see the things that have been given to us and how we can maximize them. God has given us a spirit of power to win and overcome at all costs, love that, as we work with it, it becomes so perfect that it casts out all types of fear, along with producing a well- balanced mind.

Now if God has not given us that Spirit of fear then where did it come from? How has it been allowed to become a dominant factor in the lives of so many people and the negative work it produces in lives hindering people from going to the next level and living their best life?

Is it by chance the things we are watching, or the things we have been saying, or could it be the negative but impactful words of others that have been allowed entry and have crushed our zeal, energy and excitement and next great success?

When we carefully examine our lives and the opportunities that we have missed, we know without doubt that we could have been further and should be experiencing a whole lot more. Even though this is the absolute truth it is necessary to become so focused that even from where you are you can still make things happen and begin to pursue your dreams and goals.

Laziness, abolishing this Loser once and for all.

As we continue this quest of exploring ourselves, let's carefully check ourselves to find out whether there are areas of laziness at work within us. How very often we procrastinate, often change our minds and leave so many things undone or for another day while time really does afford us the opportunity to complete them and even begin something new.

I call laziness a loser because of the wrong, bad thinking many when idle can become so intimate with and produce loss of energy, lack of drive, helplessness, feeling empty sinking into areas of depression and finally bad mouthing yourself.

May I say this if you bad mouth yourself why should someone see you as an individual Destined for greatness when You have already chosen to launch your own self attack.

Let's look at this scripture,

Matthew 25:22-29 Amplified Version

22 And he also who had the two talents came forward, saying, Master, you entrusted two talents to me; here I have gained two talents more.

23 His master said to him, well done, you upright (honorable, admirable) and faithful servant! You have been faithful and trustworthy over a little; I will put you in charge of much. Enter and share the joy (the delight, the blessedness) which your master enjoys.

24 He who had received one talent also came forward, saying, Master, I knew you to be a harsh and hard man, reaping where you did not sow, and gathering where you had not winnowed [the grain].

25 So I was afraid, and I went and hid your talent in the ground. Here you have what is your own.

26 But his master answered him, You wicked and lazy and idle servant! Did you indeed know that I reap where I have not sowed and gather [grain] where I have not winnowed?

27 Then you should have invested my money with the bankers, and at my coming I would have received what was my own with interest.

28 So take the talent away from him and give it to the one who has the ten talents.

29 For to everyone who has will more be given, and he will be furnished richly so that he will have an abundance; but from the one who does not have, even what he does have will be taken away. Amplified Version

As we carefully examine this scripture, we realize how important it is for us to ensure no level of laziness resides on the inside of us.

These young servants had the opportunity to show how gifted they were. The abilities and understanding they could put to work to get results and prove to their master that the time they spent with Him they valued, and how much knowledge and insight in business they gained.

They knew that the learning was purposeful and someday opportunities would present themselves to use all that information and knowledge they had learnt from the master. When the mind and intentions of heart are all working harmoniously, then it would become easy to know without doubt how much the master trusts them and how high his expectations are of them.

The first two servants, because of being focused and having the correct view and understanding of themselves, their master and his intentions, they got very involved in ensuring that they did not disappoint the master or allowed him to have regrets about his investment in them. They understood the importance of personal growth, personal maturity and proving themselves.

As we read the text we can imagine how he commended them that he even gave them the opportunity to enjoy the same lifestyle and blessings that he enjoyed.

23 Well done, you upright (honorable, admirable) and faithful servant! You have been faithful and trustworthy over a little; I will put you in charge of much. Enter into and share the joy (the delight, the blessedness) which your master enjoys.

Wow, it is amazing that behind every instruction there are greater opportunities awaiting, but only when we have positioned ourselves to act immediately on that instruction. The dimension of results is often hidden but revealed only after the obedience has been completed.

Now let's look at the third servant and how he approaches the master with all the stuff that laziness bred in his mind and consciousness.

24 He who had received one talent also came forward, saying, Master, I knew you to be a harsh and hard man, reaping where you did not sow, and gathering where you had not winnowed [the grain].

25 So I was afraid, and I went and hid your talent in the ground. Here you have what is your own.

Look at what laziness will let you forfeit when it's in your heart and mind! The level of dishonor, disrespect and the lack of capitalizing on such an opportunity, yet the dimensional opportunity to get to enjoy the lifestyle the master had and enjoyed so much.

Hence here comes the master's findings and payment:

26 But his master answered him, You wicked and lazy and idle servant! Did you indeed know that I reap where I have not sowed and gather [grain] where I have not winnowed?

27 Then you should have invested my money with the bankers, and at my coming I would have received what was my own with interest.

28 So take the talent away from him and give it to the one who has the ten talents.

Laziness will turn you into a different individual, one that is bitter, hard minded, one that thinks he knows all the dirty and incomplete information on his master.

It must be realized how destructive this character laziness can be and the levels it will go to make you miss your next place of advancement and better living. You can become untrustworthy because of laziness. It can also cause you to become indifferent in your behavior and attitude towards people and life.

Laziness is not just an action but it has the power to consume the mind with the wrong ideas and beliefs of others. Don't become laziness tool to be used to miss the next level of blessings and breaking forth

My indifference to reality and how life has been designed to be.

This is a very dangerous way to be and to live. I specifically looked up the dictionary meaning of **Indifference** and here is what I found:

The meaning of indifference:

Lack of interest or concern, unimportant

Little or no concern, distorted in belief and operation

An absence of inclination, mediocre, languid.

The word languid means:

Lacking in vigor, vitality, slack and slow

Lacking in spirit, listless

Drooping and flagging from weakness and fatigue

When I finally examined both words (indifference and languid) it speaks very plainly of being defeated.

Having an indifference not only about life but also of yourself will eventually send the message that you are defeated and there is really no reason to get up, furthermore to get up and fight.

It must be clear that there are certain aspects of designed life principles no matter who we are and what we have, we must live our lives, so we can fit into these aspects of design, especially the design God has ordained and planned beforehand for our lives

These life principles must be searched out and embraced so that on our journey through life, we do not waste time, neither must there be any wondering about and miss-interpretations or wrong concepts about how things are supposed to flow so you achieve the very best.

When we have the wrong interpretations and concepts of life we will try to create our own design and patterns. This will produce conflict, delays and pressure which will eventually zap all your vigor and vitality and leave you drooping, flagging, un-nerved, dissatisfied and confused when things do not function as you want them to.

Based on what your pursuits in life are, it will be necessary to ensure that those goals and dreams will mesh with the design that comes with life.

So many people know what they want to achieve in life, but they have not learnt the rules and regulations to follow, the signs to adhere to, and the way to go to make their goals achievable.

Indifference happens when you know the proper way to operate, what you should be doing to achieve the best, but refuse to do those things and then become so warped in the mind that you continue to have distorted operations and a distorted lifestyle.

Finally, being disconnected.

Sometimes people who practice a double standard lifestyle forget who they really are, the supernatural power over their lives and the destiny designed by God that they are supposed to live and arrive at by a specific time frame.

They lose focus, are distracted and become seasoned in a mindset of delusions even though they are not consciously aware of these facts. They never study life properly to realize how important it is to work on themselves, work with time and to erase the trend of making the same continued errors throughout life.

Eventually even when they think in their minds that they are ready to interact with the agent change, change is no longer working with them because of their indifference to the powers of change and their now cemented mindset. It is very difficult to bring change into a person's life if you first cannot change that person's mind, their views and perceptions and scope concerning themselves and their operation.

From this point forward, you must be very conscious and aware of the damage indifference can cause in your life and the position it can place you in. Note carefully that even though I may refer to the Word of God, these principles and way of life that I'm discussing are not only for people who go to a church or ministry, but it is for the people who want to have the best from all the worlds that they encounter during their lifetime.

I need to make this statement and I want you to take it very seriously, **there is nothing honorable and dignified when you continue to show indifference at its highest level.** Not only that but you should understand just as people watch and view their televisions, every one of us, our lives are on show whether we like it or not. It is a reality that we all must be aware of and come to grips with.

Always be reminded it is not only to public figures and great icons but even where we live, the people we may or may not interact with, as they pass us each day they will eventually begin to know our faces, know who we are and the lifestyles we promote.

When you are always in the public's eye and domain it would be convenient and proper to operate mature and wise to send the correct message to promote an untarnished lifestyle which includes and comprises of our behaviors.

Long gone are the days when immaturity and mediocrity were accepted as the normal way of life, we are in the age of pomp and pageantry. The Age when things are designed to be at their highest and greatest level, where we will send the correct messages to even the smallest child who may have the opportunity to see us on television or on stage at an event.

We must *be very mindful and serious about the kind of impact and change* we desire and must bring to our people and the extended nations across the world. It must be very clear, *we are not living to and for ourselves* but for others who need an astounding model to copy, learn and grow from.

When we have been chosen and elevated to certain levels of leadership and life we must always remember we are **chosen and given** the opportunity to make an impact. An impact that no other person has made or continues to make things greater and better and to keep history moving forward into its greatest form.

Therefore, honor must be given to the people for the choice they have made, showing them appreciation and how trustworthy you are or will become and the level of honor and respect you have for them regarding their choice.

Very often, people forget how they got where they are, and that it's the people's trust and confidence in them that allows them to make that choice. When this understanding is very alive, it will propel the necessary and acceptable operations that merit such a position.

Whether our position derives from being a cleaner, Minister of the gospel or Parliament or the senate, or Prime Minister or President, each level demands a certain level of behavior, honor, respect and protocol. That is simply how things are designed to be. To break these levels of protocols etc. sends the message that all are indeed truce and truth breakers and should not take such an oath of office or positions.

Let's allow all levels of indifference and languid operations to cease and that a new day begins to dawn where we are.

Don't be a person who looks into the mirror of God and life and the moment you turn away from the mirror you forget who you are, who you are supposed to become as time goes by and what your purpose in life is. Don't ever forget who you are even when no mirror is there!

Rediscovering Your Genuine and Powerful Self.

As you explore yourself more and more, moving through the rubble and debris that covered and hid the real you, you will finally reach that place and want to learn, grow and develop this you into the greatest and best version ever. It is good to really uncover and remove all the stuff that is there and allow new things to surface so that we can begin a greater journey in Taking the Quantum Leap.

It is necessary to begin to trust this you that is needed at this very crucial and strategic time of your life. You must believe that everything you need to work on you and to become the very best has been made available to you and most if not all of it is on the inside of you.

The more you believe and accept this as your reality the more power is made available to you to increase in all the areas necessary for getting that higher version of you out.

Properly prepare yourself and release all your personal hang-ups about life so that the internal freedom you are seeking comes, which will allow you to think beyond the norm (somebody calls it outrageous thinking). Remember being free is a state of mind and acceptance which commences from the inside first. The more internal freedom you experience, the greater your consciousness will become which allows others to see how significant your change is and then your day-to-day operation becomes very unique and attractive. *The Good life filled all the prestige you desire always follows great and glorious change.*

Acts Chapter 1: verse 8

*But you shall receive power (**ability, efficiency, and might**) when the Holy Spirit has come upon you, and you shall be My witnesses in Jerusalem and all Judea and Samaria and to the ends (the very bounds) of the earth. Acts 1:8 AMP*

I took the time to look for this verse to let you understand that locked up on the inside are **abilities, efficiency and might,** to ensure that your life will become successful, prosperous and powerful and you can have the life that you really desire that is the best life.

However, these power source attributes that are all locked up inside of you must not only be known but you must believe they are there and have them activated so that you and others can benefit from them. You might feel empty based on what's happening to you, but you are not at all empty.

It is amazing how filled you are and can be, but when no attention is given to yourself you can begin to create the wrong personal beliefs that will attract the wrong people and operations. This will cause your life to either be at a standstill or become progressively worse.

In really discovering the *Genuine* you, there will be the need to Fire, Get Rid of Those Toxic people that surround you and are in your life. It's very natural to want people to surround you, people are needed, however not those people who drain all the substance and life out of you. To really be genuine, to find that greater you that is happy, full of energy, flowing and working to create the best life, those people that leave you exhausted after interacting with them must be cut off and out of your life.

That's all there is to it. Give yourself time to reflect about your life and those individuals, look at how things are with you before they came into your life and how they are now, and you will realize that change is needed.

You must be very conscious that there are people all over the world who might seem of a certain caliber, but they are not good for you and having any part in your life.

There are many people in the world that just are good for you and will not contribute to your life journey in achieving success and prosperity. It might become hard to have to cut them from your life, especially when to others it may appear that you are cruel or selfish, but it is important to understand that you must act in your best interest, and if you don't act in your best interest no one will. This is just being logical and calculated.

Many times, when we re-evaluate ourselves, we think we are ever so honest and sincere. So to function tactfully and appropriately with people, we on many occasions play games and insert warped operations into our every practice, like telling a little lie here and there, sublimely asking for favors, and hinting how much we like the person or even doing certain favors for them that in reality are inappropriate because we want people to have ideas in their heads of how nice we are.

This behavior and practice should go, because it is hiding the genuine you, it is causing that real you to be placed at a disadvantage. You must not be labelled as a person who can't or never says no when in many cases no should be your answer. This level of operation will eventually make the trade off in your life very expensive. Can you afford to trade your happiness, marriage, destiny and life for such? Have you really examined the cost to arrive here and then to lose it all and have you seriously considered the rebuilding cost?

In finding that Genuine and Powerful you, the true meaning of what it is to be genuine must be very clear in your mind, consciousness and heart. Even though this may not be as easy as it seems it is very vital for your best and most proper existence.

When we examine and consider the many influences which exist and have the potential to become great distractions, these can affect you to the point that even though you may plan to make changes where necessary, it seems impossible. This is where you must build a high -powered absolute resistance to such great influences and magnets that will try at all costs to pull you in their direction.

Therefore, it is very vital to constantly connect and stay connected to the people who are fully charged to empower you, so you can become mature in your life walk and operations and begin to build a life based on what is acceptable according to the way of how things are supposed to be. In saying no, you are not made less genuine or selfish, it shows how grown and strong you have become.

These are some characteristics of being Genuine according to the dictionary:

1. Possessing the claim or attributed character and quality, not counterfeit,
2. Authentic, real,
3. Free from pretense, affectation, or hypocrisy,
4. Sincere, frank and open

Authentic means: **(will define in more detail in chapter 7)**

1. Being true,
2. Unaffected, being open upfront, honest and forefront.

This word affectation which might be unfamiliar to many simply means:

1. An effort to appear to have or possess a quality not really or fully possessed.
2. The pretense of actual possession.

It will become necessary to embrace the characteristics of being Genuine and ensure that daily we allow them to flow from our lives.

Being honest is not an easy stance to take but it is a very vital and necessary one. To be genuine you must be completely honest even while making all the necessary effort not to become brutal to cause pain and hurt. There must be traits of compassion and mercy even while being honest, understanding that there is a time and place for everything. This is a trait that must be practiced so you can eventually acquire the skill and art to be honest and make it your operation for life.

Let's look at this scripture,

Ephesians chapter 2: verse10

For we are God's [own] handiwork (His workmanship), recreated in Christ Jesus, [born anew] that we may do those good works which God predestined (planned beforehand) for us [taking paths which He prepared ahead of time], that we should walk in them [living the good life which He prearranged and made ready for us to live]. Amplified Version

This is one of my favorite verses in the Bible, it allows me to have a view of how great I am through God's eyes, that I can become like this in my lifetime and it tells me the kind of life and enjoyment I am supposed to have.

Over the years it has been the driving force and it has propelled me to move into many aspects of greatness because of embracing this reality and allowing the Powe of the word to work on my behalf.

We must properly understand what this scripture is saying about us. First it allows me to know with clarity that I am God's own handiwork, recreated in Christ Jesus born anew. When I begin to think about being God's own handiwork, it allows me to realize there is something very special about me that God took the time first to conceive me in His awesome mind and to go about making me his handiwork. Then to recreate me in the Anointing that I can be fully charged and equipped for those good works He has planned for me to do, before uneven got here in the earth.

Obviously to do those good works that He has planned ahead even before I got to the earth realm and to set up the paths that I should take speaks of how big and tremendous His heart is and then to ensure that I would ultimately live the good life allows my mind to accept how I must order my life and the type of being I must become to have such an outcome.

Accepting this as my reality is not very easy when you begin to ponder and consider family, status, education and all the necessary criteria that are usually required. But it is so necessary to stretch your mind and become very conscious of this reality which will open my eyes and desires to allow me to position myself in such a way that I will begin to understand the greatness inside of me and pursue it with everything that is in me.

I want you to begin to agree with me and understand that you can make your life so much easier, have the success you dream about and desire to have. Therefore, you must position your mind, consciousness and life with such poise that you will attract only the things that are great and success oriented. Your poise must send the message concerning your Purpose in life and for being in the earth realm.

You must make serious plans to live only for that purpose, having the success and greatness radiating from you so that others will see it and begin to admire and crave it. Living only for that purpose does not mean that things like marriage, kids, your dream house and all those nice things are not exempt. The purpose allows itself to become expandable and to give you all your dreams.

Therefore, it is very necessary that you begin the process of ending your days of being a caterpillar and spin the cocoon to become the butterfly so that you can begin the process of attraction. Remember like attracts like, that's what the Law of Attraction says. It is one of the most common principles and rules of life. The rule scouts out people who are of the same characteristics and behaviors and the invisible magnetic force that exists within them, moves and magnetizes them to find each other.

CHAPTER 3

Partnership

ost people have never viewed God as their Partner **(The Greater Partner, The Most Dominant Force)** working in them and with them to help and assist them to achieve what they desire in life and what He already planned and purposed for them.

They merely see Him as some Super Powered Force waiting for us to fail and then to pass His judgement on to us, or just there watching to see what we are doing without lending us some assistance. "Throw that perception of God out of your mind and right through the window, you are completely miss-informed and miss-guided about Him!"

This perception is embraced when many never take the time to consider or investigate what it is like to enter partnership with Him (God) and to be committed to doing their share in the partnership so that both parties can be amazingly happy and desire to take the partnership to other levels.

People view partnership from a business perspective and even with marriage, but many do not understand the full meaning and power there is with partnership. How it works, the benefits it will produce when both parties honor their roles and be totally disciplined and committed to make it work to bring each individual favor, blessing, fulfilment and satisfaction.

What is Partnership?

Partnership speaks of a collaborated relationship between two or more people who agree to cooperate to advance their mutual interest for the desired outcome.

It refers to having the highest level of cooperation, association, coalition, all ance, union affiliation, relationship and connection.

It also means to join forces, to team up, work together, to participate and combine forces to work as allies.

These above meanings are very powerful and mind provoking.

I know the word Collaborate seems very strong but here is what it simply means:

To collaborate means to work jointly on an activity or goal, especially to create or produce something agreed upon, and the list goes on.

In the Book of Romans Chapter 8, verse 28 the Amplified Version says,

We are assured and know that **(God being a Partner in their labor)** all things work together and are (fitting into a plan) for good and for those who love God and are called according to (His) design and purpose. **Rom 8:28 Amplified version**

This verse starts very amazingly by stating what is happening from the position of partnership. The assurance and confidence that transpires because of being in partnership and knowing what the Most Dominant Partner will be doing on behalf of the other partner. It also states the position and relationship of each partner and what will happen when the full understanding of partnership is established, believed and worked.

This affirms how we can enter partnership with Almighty God and the astounding and amazing outcome we can be assured of.

Partnership is very powerful and rewarding when you have the right partner that is totally committed to you. When there is total agreement on the plans and goals to be achieved and each partner truly commits to the thrust that each one will have their desired outcome and, in the timeframe, agreed.

The more I study this verse, it makes me wonder and consider how amazing and profound God is in all His ways and actions. He has already committed to doing His part big time in our lives and very often we are not totally committed to Him. How very often we waver and swerve from the path and no matter what, when we return to our commitment, He has never halted, changed His mind or actions towards us. He made a pledge or covenant and He is ever committed to His word and honors It day by day. The opportunities He made for us, the open doors, the favor and the list go on about God doing His part for us all the time and in a timely manner is very pronounce, things usually unfold and come together to ensure the outcome He has intended.

Look at how things are designed to work for us in this partnership, based on the scripture, but carefully note they are also designed to work for our Good.

However, with all that said, as we examine ourselves, can we say we have really been in partnership with Him, have we been good and great partners?

Have we been consistently doing our part as a partner with God?

We must ensure that the right balance is created by asking for Divine assistance that as we commit to this partnership with Him, we will become like Him and express His image, character and integrity in our partnership with Him.

Don't let us become partners who only want His assistance in achieving this grand and great life or live in the zone of what and how we can benefit from His partnership, but we never step up our attitude and position of becoming awesome partners who are trustworthy and honest to ensure each partner have their share. So, ask yourself do we treasure His partnership?

What does God want from you as a partner?

Some of the most beautiful things about this partnership are God is the Most Dominant, Skilled and all-knowing Partner, He has gone ahead and planned all our paths throughout life and has already determined the outcome we will have.

He already understands and has chosen you to be one of His partners, because He knows that you are capable. With time, if you take your relationship seriously and work your part, you can become the partner that He envisioned you to be. You must therefore believe that inside of you lies all the power and abilities needed, believe in yourself and become very involved and settled in your commitment.

Therefore, the dimension of your belief in this partnership is critical to your operation and decision making.

He needs:

(a) **Your faith** in Him for the partnership to become so alive and working. (remember belief without acting, is not belief). Faith promotes relationships, the ability to believe, it motivates and will inspire you to act no matter the situations or circumstances. Your faith is of no use if it has not done something that will bring increase and if it is not constantly attaching itself to the right things that will bring some level of satisfaction and improvement.

(b) **Your commitment and faithfulness in all areas**. These *powerful twins* start with the individual first. If you cannot commit and be faithful to yourself first, then it is going to be very difficult to commit to anyone or anything else.

Every partner wants each other to be involved but from a level of commitment and faithfulness. Just as you want to be sure they are always there and are dependable, then God requires that from us also.

Now it must be understood that commitment goes further than many anticipate. At times, commitment restricts our freedom of action. What do I mean, we just cannot do what comes into our head or behave how we want too about something or someone? Because of our commitment to whom and wherever, **we must first weigh the conveniences and consequences to see whether our actions are favorable to where we have already made our commitment. Will our actions promote the favor on our commitment or does it make our commitment questionable?**

The root of commitment is that a Promise has been made, and we have engaged ourself to act a certain way and decisions made must be considered to process what level of infringement or repercussions they may have.

I was talking to a couple; very good friends and they were complaining to me about some things they encountered. They explained to me why they no longer believe in being faithful, or giving too much and being ever so serious, because the people who you think or believe should know better and do better have their own life systems, standards and values, they say one thing, tell you do this and they do as they please.

Honestly, I was not surprised at their statement, but I was very surprised at the decision they made based on someone's position and operation.

I asked them if they understood what they were saying to me and if they realized that they too had changed their standards, values and beliefs and they could not agree with my findings at first until I further explained. I showed that based on what another individual is doing no matter who they are it does not mean you have to change who you are or what you believe, because you are disappointed and expected different from individuals.

I showed them how important it is to live life in terms of knowing what is right and making that the premise from which you believe, live and operate. You must continue to be who you are and never let how another person operates change who you are to become like them.

Being faithful denotes one being true to one's word, one's promise and vows, being steady in allegiance, affection, loyal reliable trusted and believed. Living lives that are accurate, therefore adhering or being truthful to one's standards and values. Becoming devoted, dependable and stable. Some powerful characteristics flow out from this power character. **Don't become someone or something else because of people and how they change and operate.** Being You and developing into becoming better and greater version of yourself is needed.

(c) **Total Self-surrender** to new ideas, concepts and varieties that allow our lives to be fresh, spicy, interesting, captivating, and very rewarding. Going into partnership must be a choice with the necessary knowledge and information needed and not compulsion or obligation. When by choice it is going to be very easy to surrender easily to new ideas, realizing not just the dream and goals but what is required to achieve them and the ability to become submissive and happy to redefine to use different ideas and concepts.

When much persuasion is needed to change ideas that are not workable this process can become time consuming, ineffective and frustrating.

With total self-surrender the process of moving to another dimension, operation and manifestation will make consent and submission easy. Not because any of the individuals doubt themselves or cannot contribute, but they see the picture presented to be greater, easier and effective for the dream and goals.

The lack of easy and willing submission breeds wrong motives, rebuttal, anger, jealousy, bad attitudes, frustration, sending bad and malicious signals and eventually bad mouthing. Therefore, it is very important to know the person you are choosing and consenting to partner with.

It is very true that many times people do change and can become another person because of the influence of wrong behaviors where they will forget their partnership and commitment. However, this can be beyond our control, but you must guard yourself so that you do not change and become like or worse than the individual. Don't let your inward be poisoned by the venom from others, their behaviors and operations. Guard yourself, which includes your mind, consciousness, heart and soul.

Love doing right: As the world changes and things speed up, it is going to be very necessary that we guard ourselves from being caught up in the whirlwind of things and understand how things are supposed to be in life, where you are and by protocol.

Psalms 118:16-20

16 The right hand of the Lord is exalted; the right hand of the Lord does valiantly and achieves strength!

17 I shall not die but live and shall declare the works and recount the illustrious acts of the Lord.

18 The Lord has chastened me sorely, but He has not given me over to death. [2 Cor 6:9.]

19 Open to me the [temple] gates of righteousness; I will enter through them, and I will confess and praise the Lord.

20 This is the gate of the Lord; the [uncompromisingly] righteous shall enter through it. [Ps 24:7.] Psalms 118 16-20 Amplified Version

Years ago when I made certain decisions and moves in my life according to where the Lord was taking me and the doors He was constantly opening for me to go through and have wide experiences, I remember very clearly a friend saying to me that in life you can't always live by the book (bible), to make it through life you have to cut some corners and make some moves that we think only people of no faith (non- Christians I guessed he meant people who don't go to church and believe the things I do) do constantly all the time to succeed.

He was very forceful, and I knew with everything in me he meant it. I was not sure if he really understood why he was so convinced that was the way to really achieve and become successful.

However, when I began to question him about God, asking him things like:

"Do you believe that God is a robber or a thief?" He was very adamant.

"Of course not, that's God you are talking about, how can He be like that?"

So, I further explained that if God is not like these, a robber or a thief, why would He allow me to do all the things I'm supposed to be doing, and then fail to reward me and make my life meaningful? I showed him the doors of opportunity I'm having are part of the pay back process.

He just shook his head and said

"Yea, yea if that's what you believe so be it." And that was that.

I mention this because many people, whether they are going to church or not, are of this same persuasion and because of what we put in our minds and hearts we never allow God to really do His part as our Most Dominant and Effective Partner. We literally tie His hands or put Him in a position where what He has planned for our lives is either delayed or put on hold until we are ready and prepared to receive such as we accept His plan.

As we think seriously on this partnership we have with our Heavenly Father, let us do what is right and what he requires from us so that we give Him (our Father- God) all the leverage He needs to work with us and for us.

I want to encourage you today, let's seriously look at all levels of partnerships we have and see what has become of them. One thing is very sure and certain God never left His position or place in the deal. Find out why you have moved away from doing your part and make the changes necessary to have all the Help, change, breakthroughs, money, and most of all the good life promised to us by the Most Dominant Partner, Our Heavenly Father.

Hebrews chapter 1:8-9

8 But as to the Son, He says to Him, your throne, O God, is forever and ever (to the ages of the ages), and the scepter of Your kingdom is a scepter of absolute righteousness (of justice and straightforwardness).

9 You have loved righteousness [You have delighted in integrity, virtue, and uprightness in purpose, thought, and action] and You have hated lawlessness (injustice and iniquity). **Therefore God, [even] Your God (Godhead), has anointed You with the oil of exultant joy and gladness above and beyond Your companions. [Ps 45:6,7] Amplified Version**

We must never forget not just that God is God but what He stands for and the reality of His character and his Integrity. He stays true to His character and operates from that premise. He is very right to His spoken word and will always honor His word because it is Himself and He only says what He means and means what He says.

Therefore, we should emulate Him as much as we can and take our lead from Him and not how we envision things to be or how to make them work. We must see the real picture concerning what God is doing for us showing us that if we work with Him we can be of an astounding character, reputation, and at the same time have overwhelming results that come only from Him.

This way of becoming, doing right and being right must be practiced so we can produce the lifestyle that properly gives a true and perfect expression of who we are, whose we are and how dedicated and committed we are to this way of life.

Taking this position and poise allows **The Lord to open all the Flood gates and doors of magnificent and phenomenal experiences, encounters and success.** Let's make the decision I don't just want to be right by thinking but in all our operations, behaviors and attitudes.

"To be truly rich, regardless of his fortune or lack of it, a man must live by his own values. If those values are not personally meaningful, then no amount of money gained can hide the emptiness of life without them." — John Paul Getty.

Have a code of honor and live by it. Your code of honor might come from your faith, or from your education, or from your family. Whatever the source, live by these values. Life is filled with temptations. The more you accomplish, the more people will tempt you with offers for quick gains or passing pleasures. Many men succumb to these, but those who do rarely achieve what they might have if they'd stuck to their principles. The books I've read are filled with stories of men who have resisted the urge to compromise, and who believe that this has been a key to their success. Don't cheat. Be honest. Work hard. And embrace the golden rule. (Brett & Kate Mckay)

Productivity: This comes when individuals understand what is required from them and they can give it and more.

Productive

1. Having the power to be creative,
2. Having the power to produce,
3. Being fertile.

Being productive can be seen in many ways and aspects of life but having willingness to educate yourself is going to be vital and very necessary.

This is something that we must be very knowledgeable about. God does not like unproductivity. He cannot work with people who are unproductive, people who just go through the motions without performing and having expectations to receive. That is why so many people don't have, they just think that one day, money, blessings and the good life will fall from heaven to them. This is very unlike God and how he functions.

John chapter 15:1-8

1 I AM the True Vine, and My Father is the Vinedresser.

2 Any branch in Me that does not bear fruit [that stops bearing] He cuts away (trims off, takes away); and He cleanses and repeatedly prunes every branch that continues to bear fruit, to make it bear more and richer and more excellent fruit.

3 You are cleansed and pruned already, because of the word which I have given you [the teachings I have discussed with you].

4 Dwell in Me, and I will dwell in you. [Live in Me, and I will live in you.] Just as no branch can bear fruit of itself without abiding in (being vitally united to) the vine, neither can you bear fruit unless you abide in Me.

5 I am the Vine; you are the branches. Whoever lives in Me and me in him bears much (abundant) fruit. However, apart from Me [cut off from vital union with Me] you can do nothing.

6 If a person does not dwell in Me, he is thrown out like a [broken-off] branch, and withers; such branches are gathered up and thrown into the fire, and they are burned.

7 If you live in Me [abide vitally united to Me] and My words remain in you and continue to live in your hearts, ask whatever you will, and it shall be done for you.

8 When you bear (produce) much fruit, My Father is honored and glorified, and you show and prove yourselves to be true followers of Mine. **Amplified Version**

As the world moves, times change, and systems change. **Even though God remains the same in character, integrity and word,** His methods and strategies are very updated, relevant, fresh and new to combat whatever may come now in our day and age.

Every good partner must constantly improve their level of education, thinking and operation to produce the efficiency and excellence that God promotes and to get maximum yield from their contribution.

Partnership in relationships such as marriage and relationship commitment.

Before we go deeper into this aspect of partnership, which is very serious, commitment must first begin with everyone. It must be understood that even though many people no longer take their commitment seriously, it does not mean that God has changed His mind concerning certain things that we do and speak. We must be careful not to create our own interpretation of His word to suit our lifestyle practices and think it is ok by God.

It must be noted and realized that no one can offer genuine commitment and partnership to another individual when they are not committed to themselves and their word. Even though words are used very selfishly and randomly, it must never be forgotten that our word is our bond of commitment and it is also our honor. It (Our word) denotes how honorable we are.

God shows this so amazingly with every word that He speaks. He is ever so committed to His Word, that He ensures they are manifested because they are Himself and so He Honors His word which speaks of His Integrity and Character. He cannot separate Himself from His Word.

Therefore, when we enter a partnership, whether verbally or with a contract of written words, the course of action denotes our agreement and commitment, which is to honor and ensure that we do right within the partnership. Many times, because of wrong influences from outside parties, partnership is forgotten and there is no real purpose to it.

In counselling married couples over the years, I have found that couples go to counselling from ministers who themselves do not have a clue what real partnership is all about. When they themselves have or are not honoring their commitment to partnership but they give counsel, which, is not totally based on the word of God or they give from their own ideals and beliefs.

Marriage is from God and belongs to God, however every individual must work on their marriage and make the necessary changes or adjustments to allow it to flourish, thrive and become what it has the ability to become.

There is no such thing as a perfect marriage or partnership without the individuals involved doing what is necessary to make it perfect and to reach stages of maturity.

In marriage all parties should benefit, and one should not exploit the other. I know of a couple who got married, the guy lived in the lady's house, well she paid the rent, he did not have a job that brought in a monthly or weekly salary regularly, but he was maintained well, and finally, they got married.

This lady trusted him so much that she allowed him to drop her off to work, pick her up and gave him all the leverage she thought he deserved, but did not know that while she was working he was gaming with other women, using her car and money on other ladies and people. However, as he excelled and became well known, she helped him to achieve, he continued the behavior but was open about it, because at this stage he thought he didn't need her anymore.

However, he would tell people he never loved her, he only married because of what they were building, and his actions outside were completely different from at home. He was attentive, did what a husband would do, would tell her how much he loved her, and she did the same because she really and truly loved him.

Then, she began to realize, being intimate with her husband became painful and left her hurting in her private parts the following day after having fun. She then began to study that even before they got married she would have some discomfort after being intimate and she would blame it on the hot car seat and other things that she thought contributed to it.

The shortness to this story is, the husband eventually thought he found the woman of his dreams and started to publicly disrespect his wife, people began to talk, and this irritated him. He felt people should mind their own business but, in his thinking, could see nothing wrong with his actions. However, he sends the message I'm this way because my wife has not stepped up to the plate of becoming a certain way or doing certain things. **(full story in my upcoming book Married Life).**

What I took away from all this is that people will be people and will change no matter how you feel about them or what you do for them. Very often we must be careful about how careless we can become with our lives and our partnership, the warped messages we are so unconsciously sending. Beyond that, when God looks at us, can He really trust us with His plan and Purpose to make a difference in the world?

Real effective Marriage (Partnership), if it is going to be how it is supposed to be and be lasting and enjoyable, it must be built on trust, honesty, trustworthiness, responsibility, accountability, working together as a team, and understanding how to function with one another both in each other presence and away from each other's presence.

There should be the sharing of information, knowledge, wisdom and intelligence, complimenting each other, having strong values and adhering to them and being totally loyal to each other.

Just as business partners take on this level of relationship and responsibility to achieve their dreams and goals, they go after sustainable development, find innovative ideas and solutions to take their business to another level that it becomes a force to be reckoned with and it is always relevant no matter the times, so it is with marriage.

Wow, I guess you are thinking that this is such a load to carry and to exhibit, yes, it is. However, as time goes by and both parties increase their commitment and they work the process willingly, carefully and wholeheartedly it becomes very easy and enjoyable.

Godly, good and wise counsel is very necessary for marriage so that the changes that need to occur to make marriage work can take place. Not everyone is willing to do what is necessary to make each other happy. There are some very selfish people around and when you meet them, it is necessary to watch the decisions you make. It is true you can never be too careful, and things do have a way of happening, but take your life so seriously that no matter what comes up you can handle it and come out unscathed.

It is time to work on having good and effective partnership, that requires partners who are completely focused, who can be trusted, who understand purpose, who will stay faithful and committed, have strong values that will override anything or anyone tampering with and trying to mess up their partnership with God and those we have pledged our commitment and loyalty to.

Therefore, I want to challenge all of you, it is time to revisit your partnership with God and see who has swerved from their commitment and from doing their part? Have you been staying completely true and honest to your commitment with God, your spouse and or your partner in relationship and business?

It is wrong to expect God to keep His end and you don't do yours. Likewise, it is wrong to expect from an individual what you are not prepared to give and do. Don't just think of how well you can benefit from another's life, it's time to give back and really work on creating sweet, lasting and phenomenal partnership. It's time to change these broken and derelict partnerships and rebuild new lasting and regal partnerships.

I want to encourage all today, let's seriously look at all levels of partnerships we have and see what has become of them. One thing is very sure and certain God never left His position or place in the deal. Find out why you have moved away from doing your part and make the changes necessary to have all the Help, change, breakthroughs, money, and most of all the good life promised to us by the Most Dominant Partner Our Heavenly Father.

HEY. WE ARE IN COVENANT!!!!!!

Yes, we are in covenant, we are not just partners and operating in a vacuum, we have taken this to another level. What does it mean to be in covenant?

Covenant refers to having a binding agreement with conditional promises. This agreement can be between two or more persons.

Literally, it is a contract. In the bible God made an agreement between Himself and His people in which He makes promises to His people and, usually requires a certain level of conduct from them. In the Old Testament, God made agreements with Noah, Abraham and Moses.

To Noah, He promised that He (God) would never again destroy the earth with a flood, so He gave Noah the rainbow as the covenant sign.

Genesis chapter 9:9-15

9 Behold, I establish My covenant or pledge with you and with your descendants after you

10 And with every living creature that is with you — whether the birds, the livestock, or the wild beasts of the earth along with you, as many as came out of the ark — every animal of the earth.

11 I will establish My covenant or pledge with you: Never again shall all flesh be cut off by the waters of a flood; neither shall there ever again be a flood to destroy the earth and make it corrupt.

12 And God said, This is the token of the covenant (solemn pledge) which I am making between Me and you and every living creature that is with you, for all future generations:

13 I set My bow [rainbow] in the cloud, and it shall be a token or sign of a covenant or solemn pledge between Me and the earth.

14 And it shall be that when I bring clouds over the earth and the bow [rainbow] is seen in the clouds,

15 I will [earnestly] remember My covenant or solemn pledge which is between Me and you and every living creature of all flesh; and the waters will no more become a flood to destroy and make all flesh corrupt. **Amplified Version**

He promised Abraham that he would become the ancestor of a great nation, provided that Abraham obeyed His voice and went to the place He (God) showed him.

Genesis chapter 17:2-6

2 And I will make My covenant (solemn pledge) between Me and you and will multiply you exceedingly.

3 Then Abram fell on his face, and God said to him,

4 As for Me, behold, My covenant (solemn pledge) is with you, and you shall be the father of many nations.

5 Nor shall your name any longer be Abram [high, exalted father]; but your name shall be Abraham [father of a multitude], for I have made you the father of many nations.

6 And I will make you exceedingly fruitful and I will make nations of you, and kings will come from you. **Amplified Version.**

Then to us He promised us the full package of salvation if we believe and accept Jesus as His gift to us.

John Chapter 3:16

For God so greatly loved and dearly prized the world that He [even] gave up His only begotten(unique) Son, so that whoever believes in (trusts in, clings to, relies on) Him shall not perish (come to destruction, be lost) but have eternal (everlasting) life. **Amplified Version.**

Being in Covenant therefore speaks of a Promise or Pledge that is living and active between everyone as long as they understand the magnitude of this promise and pledge and will stay committed and faithful to it.

Keeping covenant is vital to achieve the goals but also to benefit and experience the results of being in covenant.

We must believe and become serious about our lives, our word and the covenants we make with others, that we keep them alive and active, as we meet all the conditions attached to them it is guaranteed that we will live astounding lives.

No matter how we try we cannot help but to refer to God and how He is in His covenant with us. It is very difficult to refer to someone else, they may mean well but many times conditions and situations do not afford them to remain in covenant and to keep covenant. He is the most perfect and honest example and model to follow.

When our fulfilling of time covenant becomes empty, our word has no power, weight or honor and when our word does not contain these three vital power surges and lifelines then it is safe to say our lives have really lost value, character and integrity.

Very often as time goes by, when we meet other people, we forget how we started, where we were, and, in many cases, we want to disregard the life we now have. The hard roads to this juncture in our lives have been covered and now it seems it is easily sailing from this point forward and we no longer cherish how we got where we are and the aid, support and help that brought us so far. So, the covenants, vows and oaths we take no longer impress us they become lifeless and meaningless to us, but we must understand that that is not how it is supposed to be.

When we become covenant, oath, vow and truce breakers, we are certainly not like our Heavenly Father (God) and He (God) certainly knows our words are empty and we are not to be trusted.

Ecclesiastes chapter 5: 4-6;

4 When you vow a vow or make a pledge to God, do not put off paying it; for God has no pleasure in fools (those who witlessly mock Him). Pay what you vow. (Ps. 50:14; 66:13 -14;76:11).

5 It is better that you should not vow than that you should vow and not pay.

(Prov. 20:25; Acts 5:4).

6 Do not allow your mouth to cause your body to sin and do not say before the messenger (The Priest) that it was an error or mistake. Why should God be (made) angry at your voice and destroy the work of your hands? (Mal 2:7).

As we consider the above verses very carefully we want to ensure that we never make God angry by being foolish and being in folly behavior.

Therefore, let us carefully consider our actions and make plans to obey the word of God, honor our word whether it be in partnership, covenants or vows, so that we can have all the favor and goodwill accompanying these powerful lifelines.

Galatians Chapter 3 and verse 9

So then, those who are people of faith are blessed and made happy and favoured by God [as partners in fellowship] with the believing and trusting Abraham.

We are people of faith and we will build our faith so that it moves God to respond most favorably and quickly to us.

Things will change, and we will be **blessed and made happy and favoured by God as we seek to keep our partnership with God and others working at optimum level.** *Now is the time for us to see good working in our lives always.*

Remember when you give your word (get into partnership, vow or covenant) with or to anyone especially a man or woman of God, it is as good as giving it to God.

CHAPTER 4

Making Best Choices.

*C*hoice has been given to all of us, whether we choose to make the most appropriate choice that will promote and sustain the type of life we desire to live and give us the future we also desire or just live life randomly without making choices and been blown in any and every direction by the winds of time.

What is Choice?

1. This speaks of having the right, the power or opportunity to choose.
2. The act of choosing.
3. Having options and alternatives,
4. To make a careful selection.

Very often many people do not give enough consideration and thought when making choices and decisions.

Even though a choice has been given to all to personally and freely make their own decisions, it must be made very clear that immature individuals should not make certain decisions when they know they are not equipped to do so.

The first meaning allows every person to know that they have the right, the power and opportunity to choose, while the second one speaks of thinking carefully before selecting.

Too many people don't understand and really believe in themselves. Neither do they believe in the concept that there is a true meaning and purpose to their lives, and they must make the choice to discover or pursue this as a life challenge. Then there are those who believe in a life purpose. They are very excited about it but never become totally committed, serious and faithful in doing all that is possible and needed to identify it and honor it by the choices they make along their life journey.

However, they are those who have accepted the fact that there is truly a purpose to their lives and have allowed both the internal and external powers to influence their abilities when making choices. They ensure that the choices they make are going to constantly affect their purpose at all levels and allow them to pursue it and find their place.

They have found that there is a purpose to their life, and that purpose usually involves some aspect of turning their "mess into a message," or using what they've experienced through life as a means of being of service to others in turning their lives around.

Those with this sense of purpose are driven, focused, committed, and lit up from the inside. They no longer tolerate or create mess, they are not deterred or distracted from what they believe. Their vision, goals and in many cases their thinking can be so outrageous that you would tend to believe they exist from another world. They are so calculated in making decisions because one of their goals is to always have perfect results from that inexhaustible drive that offers regal and unshakeable guideposts for others to follow.

It informs them of what they wish to attend to in life, and what they need to walk away from because it doesn't support their higher purpose.

With all that said, how can one make the best choices and be guaranteed a great life?

This all starts with Knowing what you really want to accomplish in life and………….. (a) **Having A Vision** to support such. Some people are of the idea that only those who have a registered business or in many cases a place where they do business are the people who are in business. This is very far from the truth; every person's life is a business. You must realize, understand and see it from this perspective. What you create from within you that becomes external is not apart from you. (if you are selling baby clothes, computer software or equipment, it was born on the inside of your spirit, therefore it is not apart from you, it is you transferred into another area and dimension).

Your life begins from a point but as you mature and enter adulthood, responsibility becomes greater. Making the best choices becomes vital and in order not to waste time and become frustrated like every business, it needs first <u>the right vision,</u> then people to work in it to help it prosper and progress. It needs assistance, new ideas, new systems to be valid to run and survive with the strong. It requires skilled individuals and the list goes on and so does your life. Every part of your life needs these areas in place to bring out the best, think about it for a few moments. Our lives develop in stages and the more attention we give to it, supply and furnish it with all its requirements we can be assured of its success and greatness.

It is going to be very vital that every individual orders their life properly. If you cannot handle this first aspect of life, how will you handle having another business? When you realize it is beyond you seek the right advice and assistance.

Proverbs chapter 29, verse 18 says: (the first clause is what I want to show you)

Where there is no vision (no redemptive revelation of God), the people perish; but he who keeps the law (of God, which includes that of man) – blessed (happy, fortunate and enviable) is he. Amplified Version.

What is A Vision? The dictionary meanings are:

1. The act of sensing with the eyesight or knowing what you want and can accomplish for your life.
2. Having divine guidance in knowing what you're designed to be and how to accomplish such.

To make the best choices and choose carefully the path you need to walk, your vision must clearly state what your ideas, goals and achievements are. Without having this document and constantly paying attention to it, it is going to be very difficult to stay on course to accomplish such.

No matter how short or long your vision may be, it is imperative that you follow it carefully and as time progresses according to what is happening, it may be necessary to enhance, redefine and update the vision.

There must be clarity and certainty of what your Vision contains. You must be absolute and positive that these are the goals, dreams and ideas you want to make a reality, then define whether the vision is going to be huge or small, short term or continuous.

Let's assist you in formulating your vision.

The first rule: be very sure and absolute about what you want to do and accomplish in life.

What is your purpose for living and how do you want your life to affect others in every possible way that will make their lives better? How do you see yourself going through life?

Write about five goals you want to achieve in life. Make at least two of them long term, the other three short term. It will take some time but give them all together a maximum time of 12 to 18 months. It is possible they can materialize before your imposed deadline. Give the long-term goals, a maximum time of 5 years to materialize. Based on the time frame for these goals, this should give you an understanding of the type of goals and dreams you must be thinking of and the quality of life and reward they must generate.

These goals must be carefully thought about, be realistic, achievable, and the idea and conviction must become alive and clear in you. These will bring your life into a greater dimension of existence. Even if your mind or consciousness thinks it is too much and would want to slip into rejection mode, you must train both the mind and consciousness that this is what you want to accomplish and work with them until they accept and embrace them. Let them know this is your quest and purpose for life.

There must never be the thought of being intimidated because what others are doing seems more appropriate because of certain trends.

Trends have their way of changing to accept something newer and better when they are properly presented and the advantages of having or using certain things are very clear.

Very often many people are not sure of where they are going and what they want to achieve. I have met many people who are in business for all the wrong reasons. They just want to have a business to live a huge life, they never grow themselves, develop or enhance their skills and methods and when the business falls apart they wonder what went wrong.

They have not written a vision for their business or a vision statement which should clearly express the aspirations, goals and purposes of the business and people do not know about their vision.

It is very vital and necessary that you have a vision and it must be visible, very clear to understand and it must be shared properly communicatedand available for all to see. Many times, because people are very unclear of their vision they are not sure where they are going, how serious they are and how purpose driven the individual is. These same people come into people's lives and distract and divert them off the set path they are supposed to be on. Or they are not clear about what they need to contribute to the individual, whether it's more focus so that they can reach their destination on time.

Every life with a vision requires lots of **Passion** to be at work and to be constantly increasing. Passion speaks of having A Strong, Powerful, Extravagant and Compelling Feeling or Emotion that gives you drive and allows you to know that your vision (which consists of your goals, desires and dreams) will come to pass. It infuses the individual with all the needed strength to make things happen that are consistently bringing that vision to reality.

When people are passionate about something or someone they are said to be **Ebullient which means to be Overflowing with fervor, enthusiastic or excellent, very high spirited and lastly, they are bubbling up and over like a boiling liquid.**

This is how you must become about your life so that the choices you make are not just gut propelled, but you are burning with a knowing that no matter what is happening or can happen you will be ready to challenge that challenge and win at all costs. The cost will not shatter or suppress anything you are involved with. You will ensure there is minimum negative effect but astounding positive moves in other directions for greater. Any exchange must have the greatest impact in your favor.

You are responsible for growing your passion and ensuring that it is at its highest peak whenever you need to exhibit it. Your passion will become the director of your life because of the Divine invisible activity and connection connects to and will therefore order your life and assist tremendously in your daily operation.

This clearly sends the message no matter where You are, how far you have gone, with every life experience, you have learnt something fresh and new, you are still learning and will not fall prey like other people. You have grown you in many areas and have become more passionate and excited than when you first started this journey. You have not changed my mind or will not compromise your decisions, you know even clearly and can actually see where you are going, and you want it more than anyone can even imagine.

(b) You Need an Obedient spirit. This segment is going to be very short and to the point. If you are not ready to obey and act on what you are instructed to do, then don't seek advice or tell people you want to change your life.

Can you imagine the number of people who came to me for advice and when they left the meeting they never followed through on it, they forgot what they were instructed to do or someone else gave them a different opinion that they thought was better and after a while things fell apart and they now want more advice? You must not fall prey to this like many others have.

The purpose for writing this book is to assist as many people as possible who would take the time to read it and follow every instruction to their journey in taking the Quantum Leap. Move from where you currently are. It is to ensure that not just their lives change but they have the life designed by God for them and they start to live their best life now.

It is wasteful, stupid and crazy to get great and astounding advice and do nothing with it, until a crisis appears in your life. Very often you may not be seeing the advancement of challenges, but they will come at you to test your strength, knowledge, wisdom and the type of individual you are, and you must be fortified in all areas not just for challenges but for life.

You must be able to manipulate life to get the best out of it; not being tricky, sly or wicked, but to manipulate in a decent and charitable manner. Handle whatever, put it to work for you and in your favor, all the time.

In Job chapter 36 verses 11 says,

If they obey and serve Him, they shall spend **their days in prosperity** and **their years in pleasantness and joy**. **Job chapter 36 verse 11 (Amplified version).**

This verse is so powerful and shows the kind of life that every person can have based on their obedience. This is something to activate immediately in your life.

Psalms 40 verse 6 says,

Sacrifice and offering You do not desire, nor have Your delight in them; **You have given me the capacity to hear and obey** (your law, a more valuable service than) burnt offerings and sin offerings (which) You do not require. **Psalms 40 verse 6. Amplified Version**

Every person has the capacity to hear and obey instructions, but it is based on how you use that capacity given to you from Almighty God. This capacity is not given just to people who go to church or Christians but to every living person.

Therefore, make the decision to activate the power of obedience that's within you and allow that power to flow throughout your entire being, so that you can give prompt obedience and have supernatural results.

Don't think after you get advice, think before. If you have answers and already plan to follow them, then you don't need advice at all. However, if you are unsure and need directions, get advice.

(c) The Ability to listen well.

In speaking with people to detect whether they are listening to the information you are giving them, most times they would reply "I hear you" but in fact they were not paying careful attention to listen and understand the information given that they can use for their advantage. Only those who are impaired or have some level of defection cannot hear but every person without such challenges can hear but *to listen requires a certain art and skill.*

To listen well requires much practice and the ability to give one your full attention to the information given so that it makes complete sense and at the same time it becomes useful. With much practice, discipline and experience whether in the work force, meeting gathering, or even by reading and communicating with people you can master this art. It becomes an art after much practice, experience and constantly training oneself in this area.

People with sharp hearing can be very poor listeners, but they can develop the skill to master such and become active well- trained listeners.

Over the years when we were growing up at home, my mom would always say to us "the art of understanding is listening and listening well". Many times, when she would give us instructions and we had to carry them out, to follow those instructions and do exactly what she wanted, my brothers would ask her, "Mom what did you say, can you repeat what you said?" and the next statement would be "The art of Understanding Is listening and listening well". We couldn't mock her, but we would silently look at each other because we knew what was coming before she repeated her instructions. When we exited her presence, we would repeat it to each other.

The lessons we learnt were to understand and to function properly we must be giving careful listening to what is said, asked and required. You will never function at the highest if you have not listened well enough to hear and understand what is being said. Very often you will be guessing or reasoning within you whether this was said or not and chances are you can function incorrectly and make a mess of things.

Being a great listener allows you to be more productive, more knowledgeable, articulate and it allows you to channel your life in the correct direction and to limit the number of errors made. This is a very notable and desirous characteristic that not many people pay attention to. In business to eliminate unnecessary errors and cost, this art and skill is vital.

What does listening do to you? As you listen you are the recipient of knowledge, insight and opinions from the speaker whether formal or informal. As you receive the information you use your faculties of understanding to grasp what is said. What you take away from that information that can grow enhance and transform any area of your life as you remember and ponder on it, evaluate it and then see its usefulness to build your life.

As you read this book even though you have not met me face to face you have met me, because I am pouring from my heart into you to make you greater and ready to take this amazing quantum leap to the next level. As you read you will hear your voice even though silent, but you will hear my heart.

Train yourself to become an avid and active listener and see how transformed and phenomenal your life will become.

(d) Sound Advice.

Not every person has the knowledge and insight to give advice. They are some people who look through the windows of certain people from the outside of certain information to give advice when they are not experienced enough to really give sound advice.

What is Sound Advice?

Let's look at the word **Advice** first.

Advice is said to be someone's ideas, opinions, recommendations, **insight** and guidance to action. Someone who measures, examines, investigates and discerns what is needed. Someone who can solve matters, become rational and logical in their thinking and can see what the outcome of any situation will be based on their advice.

As I carefully examine the meanings I realized that there are many people who will tell you they possess if not some, most or all the aspects of advice. (but very often the advice they give contradicts what is needed and very often the needed action to bring results is never acquired). It must be said, based on what is happening, these people are still not qualified (this is not just by certification) to give Sound advice.

Now it must be very clear that I'm speaking to those who will use Sound advice for an outcome they desire. This is not for people who joke around with their lives and waste time and that of others. This is for those who are serious and understand their next level is anxiously and seriously awaiting their arrival.

What does it mean to be Sound?

1. To be free from injury, damage, defect, in excellent condition, healthy, robust.
2. Something that is strong, secure and reliable. Being competent.
3. Having no defect as to truth, justice, wisdom or reason.

And the list goes on. This is so amazing. As we carefully examine Sound Advice, it means that the opinions, recommendations, insight, discernment and guidance to action must not give me an outcome where there are defects, damage, or things becoming worse.

Hence, it is going to be very important and vital that you are very careful who you seek Sound Advice from and the relationship you foster with them. People whose character, behavior, operations and reputations have preceded them in a fashion where there are so many visible defects are people who will try to give Sound Advice, but somewhere in that advice, there is a measure of defect.

Remember we are looking forward to making the best choices. It is impossible for you to be one of the greatest mechanics around and have the worst car. It is impossible for you to give me an idea to make my life change and cannot give yourself a workable idea to change your life.

It is impossible for you to be so gifted, knowledgeable, creative and can't get your life in order and make big things happen in your life. There is a defect somewhere and we need to get the defect out because your life should speak much greater than what you say.

How you live my life, how you behave, how you operate and treat others will determine whether you am qualified to give Sound Advice that will give others the outcome they desperately need. **Best Choices begin when we know we need advice and we find the people who have ordered their ives in such a fashion that They Lead by Example.**

Sound Advice allows you to understand how you must become and will put pressure on you to do what is necessary to achieve that because you will become a product of that advice.

The pursuit of excellence at its highest form and the end of defection, settled failure and unsuccessful outcomes must in this season be worked on very diligently. We must ensure that we send strong messages that we are improving at a tremendous level and as the world progresses and moves forward to its many destination, we want to be ahead of the world moving forward to our destinations with records untarnished and very rewarding.

Find your Perfect, True Mentor that will assist you in changing your life. Remember your mentor should never be disrespected or disrespect you by forming out-of-bound relationships or seen and deem on the same level as you. There must be a huge difference, known and agreed boundaries for operation behavior and acceptance.

Finding the Assistance, you need.

Creating a vision and properly organizing it is not always easy. Also, to make that vision a reality, this is going to require some assistance and not from ordinary people, but people who have travelled this road before and accomplish outcomes beyond their expectations. This is where the greater you and all the enhancement tools, information and knowledge begin.

Don't be straddled with hesitation or caution, tell your mind to get ready this is something we will work on together and find all the right people, ideas and assistance to make this vision a reality. Always remind your mind that this vision belongs to us (you, your mind, every part of you) and we must work together in harmony to make this a success.

It is not abnormal to need help, that is why the world has a vast cross-section of people with many different cultures, ideas, knowledge, experiences and successes that no matter how minute or large, we can learn something constructive from each other to make our lives greater.

With this mindset you must begin searching for the people who are the best for what you are doing. See what they are involved in, find out how they operate daily, begin to scrutinize the patterns they have and see how they fit your equation and get busy aligning yourself to your creative pattern and path.

There are so many people that you can learn a wide variety of things from. Even though you will never meet them (meeting them could give you more advantage) or have a conversation with them, they have exposed themselves (with their personal information of their journeys throughout their life which are all about their successes, their knowledge, failures and experiences) to many through various forms of media and forums, as their contribution to assist others in making their lives greater and even more successful.

Very often people scrutinize information to give more negative feedback from incidents or negative experiences, which in some cases is relevant and can be an eye opener but they never realized the information concerning the person has been given to show them what can happen on journeys but what they need to avoid and also what they can do to have the outcome they desire. Take the information, twist it until you can find something from it to enhance and change your life for the greater.

The internet consists of a wide cross-section of information concerning anything you desire to know, and the tools are also in the information that can allow your life to become extremely powerful, successful and great.

Make plans to use these available mediums and tools to enhance your life to a greater dimension. Don't use them like many people I know to find

PROPHETESS HEATHER SCANTLEBURY

out what is the latest gossip stream about their favorite star, singer or icon but to improve, grow, develop and manage you more perfectly.

Don't sit idly complaining that I need help but there is no one to help me, it's your time to get up, get your thoughts together, know what you desire and begin to make plans to have them and a whole lot more.

Action Time.

As I grew up with my parents and had lots of interaction with my grandparents who were Pastors of a church, I was very much into reading the word of God. I had to do it because when I attended church with my grandparents you had to be able to stand up and recite a verse to show that you read and knew the word of God. Reading is a very passionate hobby of mine, so when I read this verse of scripture, I thought it related only to the word of God.

Here it is, James chapter 1 and verses 22-25 amplified version:

Be ye doers of the word (obey the message), and not merely listeners to it, betraying yourselves (into deception by reasoning contrary to the truth).

For if anyone listens to the word without obeying it and being a doer of it, he is like a man who looks carefully at his (own) natural face in a mirror,

For he thoughtfully observes himself, and then goes off and promptly forgets what he was like.

But he who looks carefully into the faultless law, the (law) of liberty, and is faithful to it and perseveres in looking into it, being not a heedless listener who forgets but an active doer (who obeys), he shall be blessed in his doing, (his life of obedience).

I always thought this refers only to people who go to church and by extension for only the word of God. In my mind I was not thinking or even realized that this scripture can be used by anyone who gets an instruction and decides to become an active listener and a doer of that instruction. That's the person that will begin to see change and sizeable change in their lives.

I did not realize at that young age that words are very powerful and always come with an instruction and to get an instruction is great, but to carry it out becomes awesome and exceedingly important.

Most people sit around waiting for things to happen, when in fact things happening are very dependent on the individual and what that person is doing. It must be very clear that this is your life and everything that is supposed to happen in it is very dependent on you and how much you participate and the involvement that you lend to it.

It is your dream and therefore you must ensure that it comes to pass. You must be involved in steering this dream in the right direction so that there is no diversion or wrong interpretation of what you want to make happen.

Lazy people, people who are unsure, people who refuse to handle their destiny and people who do more talking than producing depend very much on others to do most of the work fulfilling their dreams and making them come to pass.

I was talking to a lady and she is so convinced that her time for the big thing to happen in her life will come very soon. She is constantly saying, "I know my time will soon come and when it comes nothing will stop me," have you ever met those kinds of people?

Listen to me very carefully: it Is always your time, yes there are seasons when some things are more potent and can happen faster, but every day we live we are supposed to do our very best to ensure that what life is asking for at that specific time we are equipped to give it, so it can give back to us either now or later. We must never put our lives on hold and miss what each day has to offer, and how much we can contribute to secure the best, present and future life.

Get Up and make your dream(s) a reality, this will secure the life you want.

Never be afraid to act, it does not matter if along the way you make some errors, or you misjudge some things, it is all in the process of learning and becoming experienced.

The important element here is that you keep moving and moving so hard, learning, being much stronger more confident, more committed, more faithful, loyal and trustworthy first to yourself and then to others.

Your loyalty to **your** dreams and achieving them is vital to your success and prosperity. Increase, Growth and development must be the trail we are blazing and the trends we are setting.

The command is to get up no matter what is happening, how much has happened, no matter how weak and faint you are, you must get up brush yourself off and keep moving. Successful and great people are never deterred by what is happening or what has happened, they have one determination and that is to achieve the goals they plan and to ensure they reach that destination in a timely manner.

This must become your quest and pursuit in life and concerning life.

There is a supernatural activity coming to you by the Holy Spirit from God and it has a ceaseless supply of whatever you need (help, joy, comfort, wisdom, knowledge, peace, amazing answers to your questions, amazing breakthroughs, Divine inspiration, amazing money, provision, security and prosperity). God is never short of any of these mentioned attributes, the more He gives, the greater the flow becomes and the more exceedingly abundant the supply becomes.

Prioritizing Now!

To prioritize simply means to put things in their rightful perspective and order according to their importance.

Over the years in listening to people, I've realized that too many of them have been caught unaware concerning their dreams and achievements. Time has so swiftly passed by and now they are filled with huge regret, that it can become troubling and at the same time make you wonder where they were all the time and what they have been doing with themselves and life in general. Why have they wasted so much time doing so little or nothing?

You must never find yourself in this bracket of people. Now that you have your strength and the ability to see opportunities, you must move forward and capitalize on every given opportunity and what does not even appear, you must become so articulate and creative that you can create opportunities even out of nothing.

Over the years as I went to work each morning I already knew how my day was going to start. Each evening before I leave I would write in my desk journal how and what I want to start the next day with. The things that I did not get done that day I would consider whether they were that important and if I need to start the day with them.

In my mind I figured if they were that vital and important then I would have tackled them and ensured that they were done. I said all that to say that very often in our lives we spend so much time doing things that are not important for our personal growth and development.

Very often what another person might deem very important and necessary to another individual is not. Most times getting involved with so many things can allow you to lose focus and hinder you from seeing the little or no importance of it or them.

People only realize how much time they have wasted when certain grave and striking situations occur. Very often they are then thrown into a state of panic which eventually leads to frustration, fear and the notion that everything about them now is at its worst end.

This must never be our plight or outcome, so it is going to be very necessary that we understand the importance of prioritizing our life in every aspect and the most contributing factor to our life is all about managing our time and finances. All the others can and will fall into their perspective place as we work constantly on these two areas.

How do we work on prioritizing? A few things must be thought out very carefully. Over the years I have seen good people who were very great at ordering their lives and they became very successful, they lived and are still living great lives and the loss factor has been minimal.

Managing time is very costly and you must ensure that the cost effectiveness is not traded off for things that have more value than in many cases a price tag cannot be placed on them. For example, God and your immediate family should be very important and vital for your survival, handling, communication and the constant increase of building lasting and secure relationships with.

Very often the statement is made that God is first which is true and then everything else. This latter part is not completely true.

In putting things in their rightful order according to importance, it must be understood that God in and with the family comes first. Therefore, it is safe to say that no matter who we are and what we believe, we are not here in this realm on our own and by ourselves, it is because of the plan of God that we are here whether or not we believe and accept this as our very own reality. It doesn't matter whether you believe in God or not, the point here is God believes in you so much, He sent you here to this realm or rather He allowed you entry to this realm.

So, in prioritizing time, make time for God, which is a given and then your immediate family, husband, wife, children (this is not relatives like uncle aunt etc., they have their place, and time should be given to them). This is vital for the proper survival and constant, healthy growth of the family.

Don't just try to accomplish major success, money and fame and forget or abandon the family. I have seen too many great families presenting a non-existing happiness when they barely survived because of desertion from one party whether it be the husband or the wife. Keep the family unit strong and powerful. Time is a very powerful contributing factor here.

There are many areas we can look at when it comes to priorities, but I will choose the two most critical ones in my years of counselling that can produce serious trouble if no serious care and attention is given to them.

1. TIME MANAGEMENT:

(a) God, in and with the family. (This includes God's time. The Family is the Perfect expression of how God is and what He consists of). Giving the family, your special time, attention, love and care creates the bond and cements the security, appreciation and allows the message to be very clear how important they are in your life and how much you are so in awe at having them being a part of your life. Treat the family correctly and see the power of God move in that family.

(b) Work life. Spend time working and becoming a good steward. Using the time on the job to produce to be a blessing to the company but to increase you as you learn, enhance your skills and heighten your experiences. Know what your goals and accomplishments are and find out if you can achieve them with the job and make critical decisions when necessary.

Spend time when it is vital and very important. Avoid creating only a work life and nothing more – Red flag. Work Smart and produce more in the allotted time or in less time. Know every day when it is time to leave the office and get home to your family.

(c) Home Time. Ensuring the energy, strengths and correct perceptions needed for all are available and resident in the home. Seeing the home in order and everything working perfectly (not just people but things in the home). Allowing your presence to be felt seen and realized in the home is crucial. Setting the correct trends for your sons and daughters to pattern and follow.

(d) Your Time. This is time to rejuvenate, to become more creative with new ideas for life (the family) and to measure your dreams and goals to see where you are and what is the next move to capitalize the next level. Time for personal development, maturity, education, knowledge wisdom and to redefine, enhance or upgrade the vision for your family. (here is where your partner must be included, as you enhance you, enhance each other that you both grow together so you can both move harmoniously and rhythmically)

(e) Others: This will include relatives, friends, business partners and those who are not in your household. **Time spent here must be minimal, so it does not infringe on any of the above or create any problems. It must be understood and realized that if the time spent here infringes on any of the above it is not worth it.**

There are many more that can be listed here but I have found these to be the major critical areas with Time.

2. FINANCES: UNKNOWN AND MAJOR BAD SPENDING.

This is one of the most troubling and crazy areas to work with and on when individuals are not disciplined, honest or committed to being truthful in this area. Very often people never follow your instructions when it comes to the correct procedure for handling of finances, they operate from emotions, preferences, taste and looks.

I remember very clearly when I started to work, my wages at that time were small and I would see many of the employees living a certain lifestyle. I would complement them, but in my mind,

I would think of the day when I would be able to buy and wear some of the finest, but it never made me do stupid stuff with my money.

I understood very clearly my level at that time and worked on it until changes in finances came that afforded me more.

Every person has and can have money but not every person is equipped to handle money properly.

First, let us be clear about money, Money is not evil, it answers all things. Without money things cannot happen, people cannot function or participate in the financial system.

In my years of counselling couples, married, in relationships and even singles, the most troublesome and careless operation is in the financial realm. Not that there are no other areas but the most dangerous and frustrating is right here with finances.

Wives are very hurt and filled with anger and tears because husbands spend all the money on electronics, women or they just want to show themselves able and big. They misuse the money for other purposes and only when either the collection officer, the bank or an institution calls about the payment, then they realize how vice versa that partner has been misusing the funds.

Then, there are those individuals that must be on par with what is happening. Every new gadget they want in the home and there really is no need for these things, they just hear or see them and must have them.

So, there are some ferocious controlling appetites that must be worked on to ensure that what should be saved, invested and put to good use for retirement, education funding and preparation for an early retirement to enjoy the fruits of our labor must not be squandered.

When we reach a certain age, we should be willing and ready to take full control of our lives and begin to do the things we could not do years ago because of our children's upkeep, mortgages, insurance payments and the commitments that come with progressing in life.

We must never be afraid of facing tomorrow, being anxious or having to make decisions to work longer than we originally planned or become so dependent on the government institutions or people, that we no longer have access to our own lives, have no investments to exchange for money that we are too filled with obligations that can bring hurt and danger to us.

Agreement in the family must be a priority, this idea of hiding money, doing things behind each other's back and operating like the lone ranger when it comes to money must end, if things are going to work smoothly and saving and investments reach the potential they can.

Every detail where circulating or exchanging money should be discussed and agreed upon.

In the age we are living in women have reached a certain level that they can earn just as much money as the men, however this does not make either more dominant than the other. There are some women and men who spend wildly and never think about investments or saving, they are not even about the now and expect the morrow to provide whatever and, however.

Based on how you use your finances, will determine the life you will live and the magnitude of that life.

Finances are designed (this is based on your lifestyle) to satisfy your commitments on a monthly or weekly basis, which includes the exchange of money for services such as utilities, rent and the conveniences in the home like furniture, education, long term investments and savings. No matter how small, you should invest and save some of your money every month.

This is a discipline that you must covet and be very passionate about, no matter how small or large.

Do whatever is necessary to ensure that your income super exceeds your expenses. Your expenses must never be greater than what is earned in the home, (red flag) when this becomes the norm it clearly shows there is trouble already in the finances. Curbing this activity is urgent and it needs to be changed immediately. You must find the ways and means to turn this activity around.

Budget where necessary, don't become rigid and mean. In the meantime, live within your means and level, as you operate properly with your finances, increase will come to change budgeting, that you will have all the finances to do all you **need to and want to**.

CHAPTER 5

The Quantum Leap

This requires extraordinary power beyond the required power to take the leap but to also complete the leap.

When I got this revelation for the body of Christ and those who will do what is necessary to live an extraordinary life, I had to spend lots of time in meditation and getting the directive that will bring the sudden change that is really needed in the lives of men and women across the Globe.

This is what I was given: The time is here for the body of Christ to understand the times and age we are living in and it is the **Now Ripe Time and Age for a Complete Lifting up and out from where each individual is to a greater and more moist and flourishing place.** The current place where many are at (not just physically) but also in mind, belief, Faith, operations and Truth is too low and hence the true level of activity from the Divine, destined for this **Now Set Time,** is being held back.

I was directed that this is the time for **Amazing, Phenomenal, Astounding and Uncommon Events taking place in the lives of His people.** Not events of destruction producing fear and unrest to the people, but events to restore, replace and replenish so that without doubt all people will know that God is ready not just to honor His word, covenants and promises but to openly make a show of principalities and powers and to show them how kind, merciful and loving He is (being an Amazing Father) to us His children and how well He plans to take good care of us.

This down and out cycle, barely living, under loads of pressure and stress, He wants to bring to an abrupt and sudden end.

He (God, our Father) wants to give us the Egypt and Goshen effect and operation. While the world and nations are crying out because of recession, hardship and lack this level of activity is not designed from or by Him to touch us or even come near us.

No matter what the world experiences, no matter what wicked wealthy people set their hearts and hands to do against others, the entire move of God is for His people to take The Quantum Leap that they cannot be reached or interfered with.

The level of activity coming from Him to us surpasses what people know and refer to as the jubilee effect. This is what He had always envisioned to happen for His children and it is as if fulness of time has come for us.

This Quantum Leap will therefore require every individual to decide completely that this is very vital and necessary and be prepared to make the abrupt and sudden move in the heart, mind, consciousness and soul which will make it very easy physically.

Don't just keep complaining and saying there is a need for change in my life, where I am and with everything about me, but prove to God our

Heavenly Father how passionate and serious you are about adhering to His desire and hunger and thirst for what He desires.

All caution, reservation and doubt must go, the reality is that the set time for the leap is here and now.

Which means that each person must work steadily on building up all the power and readiness to take the leap and complete it.

Three areas that will be very important and vital for this process of the Leap:

1. **It requires the individual to be of another spirit.**

Numbers chapter 14:24

But My servant Caleb, because he has a different spirit and has followed Me fully, I will bring into the land into which he went, and his descendants shall possess it. **Amplified Version.**

Based on the attitude you are constantly working on to increase will determine the height of opportunities and events in your life. Here this verse of scripture describes Caleb as a man of another spirit.

From reading the account with him and based on the position he took to ensure that the promise God made to their forefathers, and that it was time for the fulfilment of the promise, it shows the level of qualities we must possess and work to make things work in our favor.

Caleb: The meaning of his name from the standpoint of how he believed in God and what He did is: Faith, Devotion and wholehearted.

Let's look at some astounding qualities Caleb possessed, that he was said to have a different spirt:

(a) He was of a warring attitude, had a conquering attitude, was ready and willing to fight to make what God said come to pass.

(b) He listened, believed, weighed the consequences, tossed everything up in his mind but his conclusion was I will believe and stay with God.

Numbers chapter 13:30, Caleb quietened the people before Moses, and said let's go up at once and possess it; for we are well able to conquer it. Amplified Version.

(c) His Perception and Outlook was totally different and positive. No fear, no intimidation by what they saw. He saw beyond what currently existed, He saw the opportunities that the land possessed.

Chapter 14:7; They (Joshua and Caleb) said to all the company of Israelites, the land through which we passed as scouts is an exceedingly good land.

(d) He believed the Word of God and allowed His Faith in God's promise to be his driving force.

Verse 8; If the Lord delights in us, then He will bring us into this land and give it to us, a land flowing with milk and honey.

(e) He knew God was with them, he fully believed that the Divine presence went before them, He understood what I do here and now will get Gods delight, and God will act.

Verse 9: Their (the enemy) defense and the shadow of their protection is removed from over them, but the Lord is with us, fear them not.

(f) His sight of scrutiny on the enemy and their current position allowed him to see how defenseless the enemy was so he followed the word and was granted the opportunity with Joshua to enter the promise land.

Verse 24: But My servant Caleb, because he has a different spirit and has followed Me fully, I will bring into the land into which he went, and his descendants shall possess it.

(g) Because he (Caleb) remained ever so faithful and wholly followed God, God allowed His natural strength to remain full that at age eighty-five he had the strength of a forty-year-old man.

Joshua chapter 14:6-9

Then the people of Judah came to Joshua in Gilgal, and Caleb son of Jephunneh the Kenizzite said to him, You, know what the Lord said to Moses the man of God concerning me and you in Kadesh-barnea.

7 Forty years old was I when Moses the servant of the Lord sent me from Kadesh-barnea to scout out the land. And I brought him a report as it was in my heart.

8 But my brethren who went up with me made the hearts of the people melt; yet I wholly followed the Lord my God.

9 And Moses swore on that day, Surely the land on which your feet have walked shall be an inheritance to you and your children always, because you have wholly followed the Lord my God.

10 And now, behold, the Lord has kept me alive, as He said, these forty-five years since the Lord spoke this word to Moses, while the Israelites wandered in the wilderness; and now, behold, I am this day eighty-five years old.

11 Yet I am as strong today as I was the day Moses sent me; as my strength was then, so is my strength now for war and to go out and to come in.

12 So now give me this hill country of which the Lord spoke that day. **For you heard then how the [giantlike] Anakim were there and that the cities were great and fortified; if the Lord will be with me, I shall drive them out just as the Lord said.**

13 Then Joshua blessed him and gave Hebron to Caleb son of Jephunneh for an inheritance. Amplified Version.

The above account shows that to really take this leap then the mindset and attitude have to be completely different from that of a normal person who is fearful, full of reservation and cannot fully trust the word of God or believe in themselves and their capabilities.

This special and peculiar mindset (of another spirit and attitude) must be of the knowing and believing that sudden and abrupt changes will happen and the adapting and changing to embrace to work with the changes will be necessary and vital to have the outcome.

When it comes to changes that are sudden and abrupt, it is clear in the understanding and consciousness that there is the possibility there will be no time to process or analyze what has happened, accepting and moving on with the change is the only option given. One-day things are a certain way, and, in a few minutes, things can be completely different, peculiar and opposite to the past. There are really no warning signs or actual warnings alerting us to prepare for what's coming.

Sometimes, people become so patriotic about things, they become so filled with resistance that they will want to kill and destroy when in fact things are still the same, things and dreams are killed because of not wanting to allow the Master Change to intervene and bring the desired results.

One must be careful not to take such positions and stop their lives, those of their family and others from moving into greater and benefiting as much as available.

The need for Shifting perceptions and paradigms that are embraced and believed to be concrete in regard to life, events, conditions and circumstances that you may currently "perceive" to be necessary, but have not given you the outcome you need, and desire must be properly reviewed and in many cases forgotten, given up and urgently replaced so that results can change, and life expectations become greater and are happily welcomed. It's time to change ideals and put on a whole new progressive, evolving attitude and spirit.

There must never be the thinking of regrets or allowing the mind to be thrown into a state of confusion and frustration. The mindset must understand the necessity of the changes and begin to visualize that a greater outcome will be the exchange for such sudden and abrupt changes.

In speaking with many people, they want results and big results, but they have a huge personal problem. The problem is Crossing the barrier of allowing or giving full permission first to themselves and to others to allow their minds to accept certain beliefs concerning what is vital for change and what they personally must get involved in.

The more you "allow" the faster the how and the when are revealed. Allowing and completely giving full permission disarms the resistance that keeps "heartfelt desires" from becoming "real and tangible."

2. **This Leap has a definite intended destination.**

Making this Leap at this specific time of your life will always produce the joy that can be achieved at certain intended destination. One that will enhance your life in many unexpected ways and to really position you where you should have been in life, living, financially, socially, and mentally.

Now it must be realized that this intended destination does not mean that you arrive at a destination and that's it. What this Leap is designed to achieve in your life is not just the good life of having more than enough, but to see your life transform and evolved at all levels that you will begin to understand the hallmark of why you are here in this earth realm and the experiences designed for you to encounter throughout your lifetime.

Be mindful that this leap is for all those who are tired of the same life cycles with no significant change. Those who are tired or frustrated at being stuck, delayed or barricaded in life.

Areas of the Intended destination:

Consciousness Development: Understanding the level of development that must be done with the mind and consciousness. Embracing metacognition which demands a higher order of thinking that enables greater understanding, analysis and the control of one's cognitive processes, especially in the areas of learning and development.

Fully embracing and working on understanding how the three areas of the conscience **(the unconscious state, the conscious and the Sub-conscious)** work, how to feed them, develop, grow and instruct them to work for you.

The contraction of these three areas is to produce freedom and at the same time have control to harmonize while processes of transformation, evolution and conformity are taking place. Therefore, the aligning of my internal energies with my desires becomes vital so that the magnitude of harmony working on the inside increases daily to give me all the outwardly needed results and outcomes desired.

In the Quantum cycle, there are radiant energies, designed to light up the entire internal being, allowing each individual to become lighted up, shining and bright. It is as though the brightest light bulb has been switched on, not just to light up the inside to bring awareness of what is there, but to amplify all the energies and powers to bring perfect expressions and reactions.

Personal Evolution, Growth and Image change.

Most people and especially Christians become very cautious and red signals go off when they hear the word evolution. However, if we are going to really understand first God, ourselves and others we must be constantly thinking about evolution from a biblical and spiritual process.

Evolution speaks of a gradual, peaceful, progressive process of change or development. A motion combining with coordinated motions to produce a single action or pattern.

My definition is this, desiring to use all available mediums and sources whether people and system for my daily growth and development while extracting perfect gifts and abilities from my inner self to be become and present greater change versions of myself.

To fully understand our total purpose for being in the earth realm, we must begin to evolve into higher and greater versions of ourselves, thus stripping off these old outdated, failing and trying so hard versions that think one way that have succumbed to what we say life throws at us.

Every greater you presented will have a greater outlook on life, however the attitude towards life and dealing with whatever is better and the understanding of winning ID from a development attitude and mindset.

When we carefully examine time and age, in the 50's, 60's 70's 80's and even the 90's the dress code, operation, how things were done have evolved so much that when we view these different times we laugh at them with a certain pride. We can't really believe that was how it was, and we are very thankful for the times in which we now live, the methods and enhancements that have made things much easier and aided our living to be much improved and appreciated.

The gist is, the world is constantly moving rapidly, changes are constantly taking place, greater things are being manufactured, there are faster ways of doing things to accomplish the goals or outcome desired. There are improved techniques and ways to get more out of production, and as we take time to really have a look at what is happening in the world and view it with a mind that can embrace change we will see that anything or everything that can change will change.

And as we view change we will realize that change never stops, neither has the world stopped. Your world from your position, operation and point of view may have stopped but if you were to look through your windows, you would be surprised at how much change is constantly taking place.

There is a whole world of improvement and the world hasn't never stopped at any point and said "that's it, that's enough change, I'm tired, can't be bother with no one or anything more today," no! the world moves on, technology is constantly improving and as people we must be very careful that the world does not leave us behind or is so ahead of us that we become irrelevant, ineffective and unable to participate fully to experience all that God wants us to experience while we are living in this realm.

I said all that to remind every individual you must evolve into a greater and higher being if you are going to succeed, stay relevant and make an impactful contribution from where you are to where success will take you.

As we recount our time spent in education, from when we started nursery to university, there isn't a level of our lives that has not changed. As we realize the rapid change we had to adjust and conform to receive the best training and reproduce from what we learnt.

Now, we have completed certain journeys and cycles of education from a classroom perspective, it does not mean that our learning and continual road of evolution has come to an end. In many cases and for many it has just begun or speeded up or chartering many new and different courses in life which we readily accept because we can see an intended destination. Well let's apply this same process continually to our life and see how rewarding our life will be.

Never convince yourself that you have learnt all there is to be learnt and that you know all there is to be known. The more study and time you give to more learning the more informed, wise and effective you will be in your growth and development.

As you constantly evolve and become greater and better (in wisdom, knowledge, understanding, behaviors and operations) the more your image will change, and you will unconsciously and consciously present newer, fresher and more improved versions of yourself. There are many people who have never realized or see the the need to change the image they presented. In some instances, the image is outdated and ineffective or based on their position and level of climbing certain ladders of success and greatness the image is not suitable to make the position more effective and impactful. (people can view you as a joker no matter the position you hold).

Each time you change into a greater version and have your encounters and experiences at that level, change is always looking ahead and looking out for you and will alert you when the next level has approached and let you know it is time to change again.

There is no such thing as no change even if you remain the same in weight, features or whatever there is still some level of change that is taking place even if it is backward change or what we call regression.

Anything or anyone who refuses to embrace and allow themselves to be involved with change will eventually die. The individual may not die physically 'per say', but your finances, dreams, hopes and expectations can, where you do nothing or very little and get little or no results. Things remain the same each year.

To really embrace this concept of evolution to become a greater version of your present self, the mind must be conditioned to accept this as the reality and then take the action needed. Change and changing is not easy for many people, some people feel threatened, some are frustrated, and some don't ever allow themselves to consider what can happen when there is real significant change and change for the better.

Personal Evolution allows you to see beyond the activities of where you are, the change process needed and the opportunities and results that can be achieved from change, after the process of this first stop where change has taken place.

Personal evolution, growth and change are great ingredients for a successful and great life.

The more you learn, the faster you adapt, grow and change, (personally, internally and also your image) the greater you become, your classes and masses of circles of people become greater. That's evolution and Growth.

Becoming Ascension Minded and Properly connected.

When we think of the mind we must understand that the mind is defined as "The seat of reflective consciousness." So, it is safe to understand that based on what you are constantly reflecting on will be what you will get.

Remember the mind is a very powerful and energetic tool and you must be very aware of what you are feeding it, what you do with it daily and the powers and energies you are constantly releasing in the atmosphere to make things happen on your behalf.

When we think of ascension we are looking at moving upwards and having this type of activity on a constant and consistent basis. The thinking must be whatever I am going to do with my life it must give my life a platform that raises me up and gives me opportunities to increase my experiences and eventually my outlook on life in general and my life.

The growing person will always be thinking of what their next pivotal move is that will make an impact to bring change for other individuals are not overly concerned about themselves all the time and all the grand things of life, They do not make themselves look important or let people see them in their glory days.

Please note carefully every individual across the planet wants to have nice and expensive things, they want to live well and be well to enjoy them, which is nice and great. There is nothing wrong with having all the grand things of life and to enjoy them. Every person deserves to have the fine things of life and to enjoy life.

However, when the acquiring of these things is the driving force behind what we do, how we are, that we become so ferocious (having those fine things and how they make us look, is how one view life is all about) in having them and forget what the real purpose and destiny is, then problems will present themselves. I constantly have to remind people; we do not live for ourselves but also for others.

We must go after our dreams but understand that our dreams are all connected to the Purpose and plans of God. You cannot fulfil purpose and destiny and do not have our dreams and desires fulfilled. God will not allow you to do all these glorious things for Him, and never allow you to live your dreams also, because God is not a robber or a thief.

He (God) will not own your life, use it for His purpose and glory, then to shortchange you by not allowing you to have your own good desires fulfilled. It is like stealing your life from you, and that level of operation is not God. His operation is way above board and beyond such. Your life being placed in His hands, and nothing happening to make you happy to see your dreams according to his will fulfilled, would be like God stealing from himself.

Remember the ability to dream is a God given ability and based on our connection to the divine or Sent ones what is put into our spirits and the dream realm that we peruse will find or collide with what is connected to the God purpose.

People who are ascension minded are always looking for or they create opportunities to show how skillful they are. They understand the times and age, what these two-time factors have to manifest, what they are asking for from individuals and they seek those who will take on the challenge, and they race with time and age to ensure that they are not left behind. They engrave a strong and permanent mark in life making history that no one can erase. Those coming after them will improve and take their contribution to the next level.

All the above, Consciousness Development, Personal Evolution, Growth and Image change along with become Ascension minded are spring boards to the destination of Living the Good life and having Success and Greatness continually.

3. This is where Your Real Life begins.

No matter what is happening around you, whether at home on the job, at your church or in social gatherings, taking the leap is designed to ensure that it does not have the wrong effect on you or it does not destroy or delay your next level of living and breakthroughs.

This is where your real life begins, and you must make plans now to live that life and enjoy it to the fullest.

What is defined as your Real Life?

The life where you get to live life on God's terms and enjoy life to the fullest.

Many people are so accustomed to a life filled with problems, delays and unfilled dreams, that in many cases they don't consider dreaming necessary because in their minds they can see failure, or all these big dreams not coming to pass.

Every person has different desires, likes and preferences for things and even in life. However, the common thread here is that you set your life on a path that allows you to have all that It is defined as your Real Life because when you have completed this leap nothing that relates to your old life should be happening, stalking or trailing you. You are on a new plane of living to experience the most perfect life you could ever dream or imagine.

Your real life has been designed to be filled with awesome good experiences that will bring the level of happiness and joy that the normal life cannot see or experience because they are too consumed with what is usually happening on the outside.

This statement will be troubling to the minds of many who have not developed certain beliefs and understandings about life, the bible, principles of the bible and especially God our Father creator and ruler of everything.

The God principles (Biblical) will work for any person who starts believing them and working them even if they don't go to church.

Now it must be very clear that people should find and make time for God the source of life and everything. I fully believe it is necessary to go to a church or ministry and become connected to the leaders first and then to the people. Your connection allows you to benefit from being a part of that corporate entity, the anointing and benefits that have been assigned by God to the entity such as a certain grace, flow glory and the list goes on.

They are many people who believe they don't have to go to church to know God or serve Him, which is true, but if you are learning God and really know Him you would also follow the guidelines set.

Some of the reasons why going to church is important, Church is designed to develop the entire individual (develop the person's spirit, soul and mind) to allow each person who attend to look forward to having experiences and being prepared for these experiences.

Church is designed to be a place of learning, educating and refilling or recharging go be fully charged and equipped for lif.

We should not go just to sing songs and give worship to God, get a good feeling or be emotionally hyped up. We are to be eager and ready to hear what God wants to say to us, through His word, what is in His Mind and Thoughts for us, which direction do we take to make what has been designed for that moment, to happen.

When we leave church or ministry we should be fully charged and ready to make full use and proof of what we heard and to ensure that we are constantly becoming better and greater in our learning, understanding and operation.

But they are people who just don't go to church and when you ask them why they say well based on the life they have acquired they don't see the need to and they would make you believe they got their wealth and success all by themselves working the smart knowledge they acquired. They will tell you how hard they work what they did how disciplined they were and are but they are telling part of the truth, not all.

The part they have not said is that even though they have not consciously been acknowledging God as part of their reasons for success, **God has been there all the while working with them and for them,** because they have been practicing biblical principles, God had no other choice but to honor His word. The strength, the abilities and power of movement are all from the source who is God.

Many times, people's view of God is so far off course wrong and minute. They only believe the word of God (bible) from a church point of view but when you begin to fully examine the word, it is tailored for the entire life of man to give man the life of greatness and success that will truly express God in our lives in a more perfect and real way as God is.

It does not really matter how many people are living in the earth realm, the rule of God is that all families of the earth be blessed and live the good life. God is the (Master Planner, Visionary and All Knower) One who will create and make room for all to have the same opportunity, however, it is if the opportunity can be seen and capitalized.

So many individuals are so familiar with things going wrong, even if good things happen, they are filled with thoughts and expectation of the good changing for the worse, that they never really enjoy what has happened and never release the right powers to ensure that their next level will be far better and greater to keep the happiness flowing and increasing.

Your Real life is supposed to be filled with all the great things that God has to offer and as you accept His plan and will for your life and begin to embrace this as your reality then you will see good, greatness and success unfold in your life all the time. That will allow you to experience pleasure in its most perfect form and arrangement.

Your participation is paramount, vital and is always required.

In this Quantum Leap, in quantum physics there is supposed to be a burst (amount) of energy being released to give you all the adrenaline, stamina and powers you need to make this leap successful.

After the leap to ensure that you have all the passion and fire to start your new life all over again and at the same time become so filled with excitement that the powers find your next opportunity or individual and magnetized bringing them to you to make things constantly and consistently happening.

In the below scripture look what Solomon said to the King of Hiram,

1 Kings 5:3-5

You know how David my father could not build a house to the Name of the Lord his God because wars were about him on every side, until the Lord put his foes under his feet. [2 Sam 7:4 ff.; 1 Chron 22:8.]

4 But now the Lord my God has given me rest on every side, so that there is neither adversary nor evil confronting me.

5 And I purpose to build a house to the Name of the Lord my God, as the Lord said to David my father, Your son whom I will set on your throne in your place shall build the house to My Name and Presence.

1 Kings chapter 5: verses 3-5 Amplified version.

Imagine under an old covenant Solomon experienced a type of living that was very phenomenal and interesting. Unlike what most people living right night under the dispensation of grace and final atonement.

Very often people blame God for what befalls them, but they never really examine themselves and check out the belief and operational systems they have working in them.

Hence why it is very crucial and important that you become ascension minded no matter what others may think and begin to create the life that you really want. Create from the mind set of how God is and as He is very perfect and righteous in all His ways then He (God) cannot give us anything, or any kind of life that does not reflect who He is.

Every individual must believe that they deserve to have the best life and make plans to do something for God that will allow Him to work with you to give you the life you deserve and want.

Life shows people the best way to be lived and how they can be unusually happy living in the earth realm and not be touched any longer by any adversary or evil. As we live to and for God He will ensure that our lives are far above the normal and average life. We shall live in plenty and be satisfied so that we can truly and freely praise the name of Our God, telling not only of what we believe He is able to do but also of our many experiences and accomplishments.

Based on where you live you are designed to meet the right people at the right time, have the scheduled occurrences in a timely fashion and have your life constantly being transformed, growing and becoming greater and greater.

Your best life of happiness, prosperity at every level and dimension, fulfillment, satisfaction, joy unspeakable, contentment, kindness, charity, acts of goodness, all your children knowing the way of the Lord and living this same great life where sorrow, pain, worry, anxiety and frustration become things of your past life.

Make this your quest and pursue it with all your mind, soul and spirit and you will experience this life. Conform your thinking to this thinking and allow complete and total transformation to be yours at every level and you will live your best life Now!!!

Remember, the truest and most fulfilling pleasure about life and living your real life is to not only live for you, your family, and relatives but for others. As you live your real life, open the right doors and let the people you were designed to meet, make an exchange, impact and change their lives, and as they change yours also walk right through those doors.

Be mindful, living your real life is not just a matter of being conscious about it but a matter of choice. Choose wisely.

CHAPTER 6

Money, Success and or Growth?

All three of these are very vital and necessary for life and enjoyment. You can have all three of these in your life to ensure you live your best life now and experience all that you are designed by God to experience throughout your lifetime.

Each waking moment remind yourself of this, **I deserve the best life as I make God happy and give him pleasure out of my life, He will in turn give me the unusual life.** Let this become a knowing by believing and accepting this as your goal of reality.

What is money? Money is the tool we use to make points of exchange whether for goods, services or investments. The dictionary puts it like this Any circulating medium of exchange.

Not many people see money from this concept, of making an exchange. When you listen to the news and in speaking with individuals, they refer to the use of money as spending, which is incorrect because as you use money you get something in return even if the value from your perspective is lower.

Therefore, we must never make comments like money is bad and evil and too much money will turn people into different individuals. Truthfully, money only has a label based on whose hands receive it, and the relationship individuals have with money on a whole.

Put this in your mind and know, "There is no money shortage in the world. Not where you are and where you want to go."

Recession, tightening the belt, cutbacks, layoffs, withdrawals and all these amendments are presented to discontinue the opportunity for some people to live well, all these deflated economic sanctions and activities are there to subject the mind and eventually the entire individual to lack, pressure, poverty and constraint in living which is against the rule and plan of God.

Restriction, lack, Poverty and restraint will lead to life being drain and the working of the death cycle whether physical socially, mentally spiritually, or psychologically.

Having this knowledge of the strategic plan of governments and other entities working against people experiencing the very best, it is very vital that we understand our relationship and handling of money is critical and ensure that our operation becomes very honest and above board.

Having money or the access to money is very important, it allows everyone who either has or has access to it to be able to participate in the financial systems which will either enrich our lives and others or cause our lives to be stagnant until there is no more participation in the area.

When there is participation, there will be levesl of activity that gives you much more experience, and it allows you to become more developed into the handling and using of money properly.

The proper view of money and how to handle and use money is to understand that you are constantly making the exchange of one thing for another. We exchange money for utilities, food, clothing services and the list can go on. What we must be conscious of, is that the exchange can and should be limited to needs and not also wants until we are at the level and secure financially to do all we want to and to engage any system.

Very often, people are fully aware of their income, but many of them do not live within such and where necessary budget for the needs and allow their wants to wait for the appropriate time when influx and abundance is present that they can attend to their wants. This operation can and will eventually create problems.

So, how do we use our money? We must start from the premise that our expenditure (money to exchange out) must never be the same as your income or exceed it. When this is the case you will eventually be in trouble financially.

Also, if you really want to ensure that money keeps following you and stays with you, you must use your money properly by exchanging it for your necessary needs. Train your eyes and heart to accept certain money principles for living and do not allow yourself to live in a world that everything you see and desire you must have.

Things are constantly changing and as you participate in the financial system properly you will eventually have all the money you need and want, to live well, be well and do well. You should never use your money unwisely, (which will create unfair exchange which is, I see it, I want it, I buy it, but really don't need it). You need to invest now to live on in your latter years. Most people who have experienced the lack of money at some time in their lives, usually participate in the financial system very improperly.

They create un-necessary debt, that they never attend to, their games of exchange are very in-appropriate and in many cases, based on competitive behaviors where they create false perceptions about having money, they are eventually shut out of the financial system with little or no participation.

There are many people who say they don't love money and today they need it in a tremendous way, and no matter what they do, money comes, and money goes just as fast. Every person loves nice things and desires to look nice, which is great. However, money knows and studies its handlers and knows how the handler is, what they are becoming and then money has no choice but to react accordingly.

We use our money to make the exchanges needed, we pay our bills (exchange): we need and use the services, we pay up and pay up on time, we must never decide it does not matter let me miss the payment, in truth it does matter, the silent messages you will send to money, I (the handler) am very irresponsible where fair exchange is concerned and at the same time money knows I should not be in the handlers' hand right now, I am due to be in another's hand.

Even when you are not on a budget per se you should be very alert in the exchange of money where needs are concerned over wants. **It is vital and**

very important to distinguish what your needs are between your wants. Mark this very well, your needs must be attended to first, while your wants can wait and be attended to later.

No matter how little or much we earn, we should ensure that we use our money very wisely and make exchanges that will eventually profit us and our families, which means that we must save some of it no matter how small. Small things have a way of becoming very big over a period.

I've met many people especially women who complain and say how little their money is, and it does not allow them to save anything from it, but that is based on having their expenditure exceeding their income, which will always create problems and will not allow them to be able to understand or try to make their money work for them.

It is very important that you work with the money from where you are now. If you handle your money well, things will change so rapidly that you will be so surprised at the open doors money will make available for you.

Using and working properly with money to get the level of success and results that money can bring requires a disciplined and mature person.

Discipline from the understanding I could buy everything now but are they necessary, do I really need them now or can they wait until another time.

Mature I can replace that with something else I already have. No need to spend because of the occasion or based on what others are doing.

The attractions to the good life and having nice things are so great that when an individual is not disciplined and mature they will be constantly getting rid of money, instead of circulating money for the things they need, and then end up using the money that has been targeted elsewhere.

Don't be fooled, the attractions are so huge, and it is like they have a very strong voice, which is constantly calling and at the same time seducing people to forget where they are financially. (Don't be too concerned about your level and the people who tell you work your level until it changes and wait on it, it will change), just use the resources you have, life is made for enjoyment. This level allows you to be seen, heard, talked about and be accepted but the longevity of this life is usually cut short because the maintenance is high and the bank account (resources) cannot sustain it.

The more you work the level you are presently at, (using your money and other resources properly), you will increase yourself personally, your money and resources so that the wisdom needed to handle and even increase it will come and work so awesomely. This will cause time to speed up and change the level to smoothly take you to other levels until you have reached the ultimate level desired.

Therefore, don't be highly motivated only by money, or don't just make that your primary focus. This can cause you to be so distracted that the things you need to be doing, the meeting you need to be having can become so secondary that they never happen in the time frame allotted to them.

As I meet many different types of people, there are those who make things or create ideas because they want to make more money, and they are constantly looking for ways and new concepts to produce more stuff that they can have more money. Some of them are not too interested in what they produce, whether of quality or not the driver there is making more money.

However, I like the concept that Walt Disney shares with all his viewers, "We don't make movies to make more money, we make money to make more movies."

In essence, the love for money is not just to make more money for oneself but to be able to expand oneself by the services or products you are offering. The need to be constantly driven to produce higher and greater quality must be in you. Which means that money is not the mere motive but the areas of evolution, constant development, not racing with time, technology or destiny, but to be always ahead, relevant, and blaze the trails and direction for others to follow.

Don't be motivated only by money and success for personal satisfaction and having all the external things that allow people to see grandeur. Strive to be highly motivated from the inside out to ensure that your life has its full purpose at work and that you are moving through life driven by purpose, always evolving, rebranding and upgrading personally where necessary. Also, the services and products that we offer within our organizations will always reflect who we are and how we think.

One of the greatest things we must guard against **is the fear of having too much or too little money.** Based on where we are going and the things in life we are doing, how we are handling life will eventually allow money to come and flow to us in abundance.

When you have accepted the true purpose and understanding of having money and its purpose and usage as part of your consciousness and reality, it will release all the fear and anxiety of pressuring yourself about getting them now without working all the processes that will bring them to you.

Many people make you believe that they have worked so hard and by working hard, their achievements are the results, but they forget to instill or reveal to many the invisible power and tools, (working hard maybe a part of it) that are constantly behind their hard work and long hours to accomplish and achieve their goals. Truth be told, without the invisible power and tools at work with them and for them they could never achieve.

Ultimately, it is truly the invisible power tools, power force and power source that bring these accomplishments.

Success: What is success? The dictionary meanings state the following:

1. The favourable or prosperous termination of attempts or endeavours; the accomplishment of one's goals.
2. The attainment of wealth, position, honours, or the like.

The meanings are true, and I am sure that many can say they have conquered and experienced the above, however:

My definition in looking and carefully examining Success goes way further. It is the ability to use the internal power to conceive and birth ideas, pursuing the concepts and tools to make those ideas a reality that will affect people and silently speak to people to allow them to believe in themselves and the power to accomplish any goal they want. The ability to empower others from where they are to where they need to go.

Personal success is not just about one attaining for themselves. No matter how we go about achieving our own success, we will need the assistance of others to achieve it. However, while we are in pursuit of our personal success we release an invisible power to work with those assisting us to find their own success and be conscious and serious about having it.

To achieve success, it is not so much about how many great and astounding ideas a person can conceive, birth and talk constantly about, but it is all about moving those ideas from being ideas to the actual thing being in progress and materializing.

Hence, I refer to the quote made by the famous Michael Jordan, the basketball player, "Some people want it to happen, some people wish for it to happen, and others make it happen."

Success must be in the mind and must also consume the individual so much that they have no other choice but to focus and work steadily on that idea and make it a reality.

Even though we made Growth the very last one to discuss, this is the most critical one. We must scrutinize to see where we are, what's happening with us, so we can make the changes and be on our destination.

Growth: What is growth?

The dictionary defines: The process of growing, full development; maturity, An increase, as in size, number, value, or strength.

The process in taking the quantum leap to greatness whether it is for business, marriage, relationships or personally will require lots of personal growth.

To do well and take your money, success and life to each next dimension there must be the ability to reach, to explode where you currently are which will require that each individual plant in their mindset the importance of growth. The more you grow yourself personally then it will be easier to grow your money and success as you use the internal powers to make your life and the life of others astounding.

Always remember, that as time goes by everything grows. The day gets older and the time gets later each day, even though we may see many midnights and brand-new days giving us the same time and name (e.g. reaching One o clock on Wednesday will not stop you from reaching one o'clock on Thursday). One thing is very sure, the date changes so we are constantly, whether conscious or not, seeing the days get older and the age becoming older even when they offer us new ideas, technology or greater purposes for living.

2020 has gone, it's not coming back 2024 is here and will soon be gone, that too is not coming back.

We must realize to function at the minimum level still requires some degree of growth, so imagine functioning at a greater and more impactful level, look at the quality and quantity of growth needed to do well and to achieve faster and greater. Begin to imagine the levels of achievements that can be attained.

Anything or anyone who refuses to grow will become irrelevant, frustrated, bored and very disinterested in what is happening. They will even miss seeing what is right before their eyes because the mind is slowly closing shop and the mind and spirit have no motivators at work.

Time and life are all about growth, development and maturity. We must use our senses very carefully to take all the advice given to us by time and as time goes by and matures, ensure that we are like time, always moving and presenting opportunities.

Growth must never be traded for anything in your life where life, success and achievement are concerned.

There are some regal elements of growth that every individual must take the time to study, not reasoning but to consistently work on having them cemented in the mind and knowing with surety that your existence is embedded in these elements.

Evolving growth requires each person to learn and truly understand themselves, know who they are, their abilities and capabilities and unite with the internal powers so they become one with themselves and allow that internal power to be so magnified that it changes the external.

This level of operation functioning at its greatest requires a high level of understanding, wisdom and knowledge about oneself and what can happen when levels of growth constantly take place.

This shows the separation between the folks who have the correct view of themselves at different levels and want to ensure that those views or dreams or imaginations become a reality, and the folks who just don't believe or imagine that they can attain such in life and give life the knock it needs to respond favorably to them.

Very often people say they don't believe in God and they chant their existence from a separation mentality that God is somewhere in the sky. He is considered as a big giant or power who is just watching over us and waiting to rain judgement. When certain unfortunate situations befall many then the anger is loosened and directed to **this God in the Sky.**

What must be understood that the God that we considered to be in the sky is truly the God that lives on the inside of us and because of not evolving and learning oneself, we very often live in a reality that has no real truth about ourselves and definitely about God.

Whether we believe in God or not He is already living on the inside of each one of us, the problem comes when the knowledge base of each individual has been left unfertile and unexplored then the acceptance and embracing of certain truths and realities never happen and therefore the scope of life becomes very normal and usual.

One thing is very sure, whether we believe in the existence of God in our lives, **He surely believes in us, because He not only lives on the inside but allows powers that are connected and comes only from Him to work for us.** We could and will achieve more when we submit, yield and totally surrender to these powers to create harmony that we can embrace and experience a greater existence like men of old experienced.

To magnify what I'm saying, whose power is at work to wake us up each morning, giving us strength to move and go about our daily routines and to accomplish each day? We cannot exist and survive on our own. We don't possess such abilities by ourselves, we have them because they have been freely and graciously given to us, to allow us to live, move and function in Him and with Him being the engine of our lives.

To really reach our highest and greatest potential, and really do well to soar through dimensions and levels of accomplishments, growth is vital. Many people when they reach a certain level of fame because of no growth, their lives fall apart, and they fail. Many great stars because they never mature to the level of acquiring fame and other levels of attainment when certain challenges presented themselves they resorted to the wrong methods of handling the challenges which ended their career or they fell from certain levels and never regained their position.

Finally, we need all three of these, Money, Success and Growth for our lives to be exceptionally better and to be a great blessing to others.

All are vital for successful living; the secret is to ensure that all three parts reach their maximum level that the balance can be always there.

CHAPTER 7.

Having the Advantage.

What is the meaning of having the Advantage:

1. Special favored for quick Success.
2. Elevated to the position of superiority.
3. To quickly and easily advance further.

Therefore, having the advantage will enhance your core behaviors which allow you to show how brilliant and creative you have become and affect your position of Superiority. Having Th Edge.

What are core behaviors?

The word core refers to:

(1) The most essential parts of anything.
(2) Of central importance,
(3) The fundamentals of how things are supposed to be.

And what are behaviors?

Behaviors refer to:

(1) Observed activity in humans or animals.
(2) The action or reaction of someone or something.
(3) Actions usually measured by commonly accepted standards.
(4) The conduct of an individual.

What are core behaviors? They are behaviors that allow individuals to personally review their lives, begin to make the necessary changes to become more dedicated and committed to themselves and to ensure that their lives have more meaning and purpose to what they have been marked to produce in their lifetime.

They exhibit actions that will shape the world in a more positive and unique way, they have studied what the future is demanding, they are not just existing in the present but they are constantly equipping themselves to produce what is demanded. They understand the need to guard and protect their dreams, how important it is to keep them alive to see the reality of them. Therefore, they engage with the people who they know will assist them in making change, while at the same time they themselves are being transformed in all areas while allowing that same process to take place in the lives of others.

Therefore, it is very clear to understand the level of behaviors we must be ready to display that will allow us to have the advantage and qualify how intelligent and wise we have become.

This really refers to being so very mature that we have upgraded our behaviors to mesh with where we are going and the greater level of life we are in pursuit of. It also shows and denotes how knowledgeable and inform they are but have adjusted everything to be a force to win and succeed in all areas.

Now in the text here,

Gen 12:1-4 Amplified Version.

1 NOW [in Haran] the Lord said to Abram, Go, for yourself [for your own advantage] away from your country, from your relatives and your father's house to the land that I will show you. [Heb 11:8-10.]

2 And I will make of you a great nation, and I will bless you [with abundant increase of favors] and make your name famous and distinguished, and you will be a blessing [dispensing good to others].

3 And I will bless those who bless you [who confer prosperity or happiness upon you] and curse him who curses or uses insolent language toward you; in you will all the families and kindred of the earth be blessed [and by you they will bless themselves]. [Gal 3:8.]

4 So Abram departed, as the Lord had directed him; and Lot [his nephew] went with him. Abram was seventy-five years old when he left Haran. **Genesis chapter. 12 1-4 amplified version.**

What is so amazing in this scripture is not only the instruction of understanding the timing to move away from his relatives but the reason for taking such course of action. God allowed Abram to know this moving away is going to give him the advantage and look at what the outcome will be of Abram's life and certainly that of all those who will be with him and supports him.

It is very clear you must be willing to follow any instruction given even though it might not necessarily seem appropriate or even within your scope to understand and study. There must be the willingness to believe what you hear, promptly obey the instruction and if necessary visualize what your life can become as you make the first step in that direction.

Let's dissect this text: Abram will have the advantage and look at what having the advantage does in a persons' life.

(1) I will make of you a great nation.

(2) I will bless you with Abundant increase of favors.

(3) Your name will become famous and distinguished.

(4) Being able to dispense good to others.

(5) Those who confer blessings and prosperity on you God will bless them.

(6) Those who curse and oppose you, God will curse and oppose them.

(7) In Abram shall All families of the earth be blessed.

What is so awesome about having the advantage is that you get to have a relationship, ministry and message to the entire world, to affect it in such a positive, exceptional and meaningful way. Giving you the opportunity to touch lives around the world that you would never dream possible. A super gigantic purpose.

Very often when people are thinking of becoming great and successful they only think of their families (which includes the immediate and extended). However, in the mind of God, He wanted Abram to have the mindset of building people into becoming a nation but one that would become great and understand purpose and reason for being in the earth realm.

Having Abundant Increase favors allows me to visualize the people that God would allow Abram to meet and whether they liked or favored Abram, because of God being with him, they would have to operate with Abram showing him abundant favor. Have you ever taken the time to think about God putting the right people in your path to show you all the favors you need to get you to the next level of success and Prosperity?

Then it continues to advise of how his name (Abram's) will become famous and distinguished, goodness, not just famous but also distinguished, which tells there is going to be something very unusual but potent about Abram's name. Distinguished in such a way that it brings hope and allows me to believe that my name can also become like his as his spiritual offspring if I am willing to do what is necessary to make it happen.

In the world today, there are so many people who really need some goodness and good things coming to them to change their lives and to allow them to have the opportunity to live life at a greater level. To prove to them they are not destined to fail, were never marked for failure. It's time for us to be so empowered in all aspects of life that we can dispense good to others wherever it is needed. The light of understanding must be so bright and alive in us that we are not in the earth to live to and for ourselves but for others to serve them and give them the life they desire and deserve.

Abram did not live in the place of being afraid, hesitant or threatened by what other people were doing. He understood the promise that was made to him and He believed until he became fully persuaded that God would be faithful to His promise, so he just took his position in functioning how he should be and this he did. He understood when God said to Him I will bless those who bless you who confer blessings and prosperity on you and curse them who curse and oppose him, he knew that God had set up people to bless him and to always move him (Abram) to greater levels of living and existence in the earth.

It is very important to know and believe that the operation God set up for Abram, He (God) has that same operation attached to your life, but you must believe such and find out what is your divine specific instruction, begin to obey it and see your life totally transformed because of having the advantage.

God's intent for Abram in having the advantage, was to ensure that Abram's life was exceptional and from generation to generation, Abram would become an icon because of His Faith and relationship with God.

With Abram having the advantage, it allowed Him to affect his time, people, the age and even ages to come. This can also happen to all those who have the advantage.

Always be conscious that when in certain areas and situations even if the advantage is not offered, your vision and awareness must be at its' highest peak to spot opportunities of taking the advantage and you must capitalize in doing so. Taking Advantage.

Exploring New Terrain.

Having the advantage allows you to become so creative, powerful and full of so many ideas; but to really produce dimensional greatness from having the advantage it will become necessary to explore new terrain, find and seek out what the age in a few years will be like, its demand and begin to learn those things to affect the terrain.

Terrain here in this text must not be subjected to just a piece of land, but spread your imagination to territory, places, buildings and even people. This is necessary because the mind and consciousness have embraced the fact that there is a world-wide ministry given to the individual because of having the advantage.

There is a very famous and regal statement made by the young and Successful Mark Zuckerberg the Cofounder and CEO of the social media Facebook and it says:

"My hope was never to build a company; I was driven by a sense of purpose to connect people and bring us closer together."

I was reviewing this statement and it became so profound to me, imagine how He was driven by a sense of purpose to connect people and not just people, but people of different nationalities, backgrounds, race, creed and color and my goodness, look! it worked. He made it happen. Look at the greatness of this social media platform where location and time zones are no longer barriers to make connection and interact as often as desired.

They are some requirements, and I know that many have used this forum for the wrong purposes, but beyond all that the intentions and the influence of this sense of purpose to give every individual the opportunity to explore new terrain in making connections and even building lasting relationships and establishing new relationships has become awesome and very exciting.

Exploring new terrain gives the opportunity for people to view each other differently and change mindsets and perceptions and to break down or close barriers and cultures that no longer need to exist. It affords the ability to promote different cultures, allow all levels of people to meet each other, build their lives by learning from ideas and concepts that can be harnessed and learnt from this media.

The exploring of this new terrain must first begin with you where you can find a new version of yourself to start out on this journey. The understanding is that while I am on the quest for Greatness and great things then I will personally begin to make all the adjustments, adaptations and transitions necessary, that when I begin to move in the advantage nothing holds me back personally.

It must be understood that the time has come for leaving behind or eliminating all the people and things that have hindered the flow of the advantage working for you. Therefore, you must begin to leave old operations, old ways of things working and accepting a new upgraded way of effective and easy operation. The normal and old way of life and its operations have contributed to your unhappiness, low achievements, being unfulfilled, financially raped and seemingly boxed into a place of hardness.

The purpose of exploring other terrain is to affect and impact your life to the extreme to bring substantial and lasting change and results you so long for. To make such an impact it will be necessary to find your personal special niche and affect it at every level and dimension.

Always remember that terrain is also referred to as new levels and dimensions that will enhance and solidify everything relating to ensuring that you have the advantage.

In climbing to other levels, believe that the opportunities to have the best and the greater will come, filled with all the happiness, joy, fulfilment, satisfaction, money, homes, jobs and completeness, they all exist at the next terrain of your life.

Becoming Unstoppable.

As I study more and more about having the advantage in my life, I came to the conclusion that the Advantage can be referred to as **A huge tremendous highly skilled Master** who has knowledge and wisdom of everything concerning me, and is willing to ensure that all other systems work for me to give me what I desire in life and from life according to the will and plan of God for my life.

Therefore, I must always be at my best and work cohesively with the advantage of ensuring that the strategies he is bringing to me I am prepared to understand and accept them even if they are unheard off, to keep achieving the best results he is bringing me.

From this point in my life I must believe and know with certainty that the Advantage will speak to the Law of Attraction and advise it (the Law of attraction) of only the people that I must meet who are in purpose and understand their purpose for coming into my life and will assist me to make significant and astounding marks in life on my journey to each destination.

Even though the law of attraction has its own principle where like attracts like, it cannot bring into my life from this point onward anyone who may be thinking or pursuing greatness but might be unsure, delayed, distracted or not totally serious. It understands the message from the advantage and will find only the correct and perfect people for me because the advantage has advised the law of attraction: I must have perfect actions every day of my life and perfect outcome and they must be timely. Hence making one Unstoppable.

It is as Napoleon Hill makes it absolutely clear every Unstoppable person must be working to achieve the MASTERMIND PRINCIPLE. This principle consists of an alliance of two or more minds working in Perfect Harmony for the attainment of a common goal or object. He further states that no two minds ever come together without a third invisible force or power which may be likened to a third mind, which is the Divine Power (The Advantage) at work.

As I understand this activity coming from the Divine, I will not waste time trying to think hard, or be under any pressure, I constantly feed myself with more knowledge and I also feed the advantage with agreement and unity and I position myself to allow Him to cause me to stand out above all others as I flow in wisdom, knowledge, abilities, efficiencies, might, astounding strength and capabilities.

Even though all of this is happening I am at the same time enjoying my life and looking forward to any challenge that would want to arise. My life has become so meaningful, I'm not only infused with strength and energy for all things, but the continuous heightened excitement keeps me going as I am constantly anticipating the next victory and phenomenal win.

Being like this creates the platform for others to dream and desire this level of being and living. Not every person is ushered to such a place and stance in life, however, everyone can achieve this but when considering the process and work required to do for their own benefit, not many are not willing to pay the price in going so far, working the process profusely or in many cases be labeled while on the journey of becoming unstoppable.

Many times, the people who are in this pursuit are very often thought of as people who are crazy, from a different age and world or even living in their own world. Those who scrutinize them never take the time to find out what are their drivers and what is going on in their heads. The people who are in pursuit of their dreams understand the value and purpose of time and living. They have set themselves to etch their names in history and they understand that this requires a brilliant mind to produce something of its own kind to assist humanity to the next level of ease and living.

Nothing is ever too hard or impossible for unstoppable people. They live in a zone where they believe that they are not hindered or affected by what other people deem impossible or hard. Everything they do is a result from the high thinking patterns and molds created in their own consciousness and mindsets. Challenges are never a discouraging factor, they see and deem them as perfect time instances to either sharpen areas of skillfulness or its time to create something greater.

Each time they move through another dimension they are constantly losing the previous mindset for a greater and more expanded one. As they expand their minds to see what the next uncommon thing is they can produce or create, purpose is constantly showing them the types of platforms they must be building to attract the right people whose performance will enhance the value of those platforms. At the same time, they will force other people to recognize that they too can get into the race and so they respond by going after their dreams while finding the tools that will develop them in such a way.

You must believe that everything you need awaits you. Some things are locked up on the inside while all the people you are destined to meet who have some of the tools you need are awaiting your arrival at certain destinations, so they can easily and quickly make the exchange.

Unstoppable people don't only have the mindset that they cannot be stopped or that they are unbeatable, but their drive is to constantly and always evolve to find in themselves greater and surpassing knowledge, concepts and ideas that keep them on the leading edge.

They understand that even though they might be considered by others to live in a world of their own they are at the same time bringing an influence that will challenge those in their world (just settling or doing the normal thing, or just accepting little change) to exchange where they are for something far better enhancing and life changing.

They can see very clearly the need for change and they can even read the times to know when it is time to allow the present world, age and certain levels of existence to fold up as they are no longer valid and changeable for the present or future times. Creating the world that everyone gets to share in and to receive a piece of the pie is far more satisfying for them than being seen as great and unstoppable. Every life must be affected in a great way to experience how life should be lived at its highest desire.

Here are some of the Profound characteristics these unstoppable people possess, guard, protect and magnify to ensure they give them maximum service.

1. **Authenticity:** They are genuine and real; they have an orign of unquestionable belief and internal evidence supported by their own trust and acceptance. They represent true nature and will not change how they believe because of the Divine Internal powers at work in them. They are constantly working on staying reliable, trustworthy and profound in all things. They are not afraid to show who they really are whether it is their strengths, accomplishments or flaws. They have the conquering mindset to work on all areas to produce only the greatest and most excellent. Their

way of life and lifestyle inspires a renowned trust which allows people who interact with them to become comfortable around them, learn from them and even voice what they think.

2. **Integrity:** As they allow their honesty and trustworthiness to be seen in both their behavior and operation, they create for themselves and impeccable integrity that will command respect, honor and pride not only in their work or themselves but also for others, and people will exhibit these same qualities to them. Without having to do much, people understand how they must function with them to learn from them, acquire some of their skills and in many cases, order their lives more carefully instead of being careless and irresponsible.

Authenticity and Integrity foster trust and keep it alive and functioning.

Many people do not understand the importance of having integrity and how characterized they are when integrity is functioning at its highest level. Integrity must not be optional but of vital importance to one's perfect existence and greatness.

3. **A Good and Sound Ego:** when I was thinking about ego I started to smile because most people when they speak of people who have egos they often respond from a negative place. When there is success and things are working out well it is normal to feel extremely good about them and that feeling can and will put anyone in a better frame of mind so that sometimes people never understand why the individual is the way they are. Mind you, I'm not forgetting that there are many people who are in high places that are very arrogant and annoying, and I'm sure you know a few.

It is very necessary to have a good and sound ego. This literally shows how confident you are about you; you are very positive and sure of your decisions and can trust your opinions and judgement. This confidence is really connected to how authentic you have become. It shows how considerate you are, able to listen to other opinions and weigh every opinion accurately and where necessary make changes accordingly. It promotes a radiating strength that many people would think twice before displaying such. People who have built this type of ego (good and sound) are not afraid of what they have achieved and have become, they are very comfortable in their own skin. They understand and adhere to protocols, they are constantly improving themselves and have become responsible and accountable first to themselves, God and those who they serve and influence.

4. **Efficiency:** Unstoppable and Astounding people are no longer striving to be just good; they have crossed all conquered barriers to become efficient and proficient in all areas of life. They understand the type of message they must send to the world, the image, ideas and perceptions they must plant in the minds and hearts of people and they make this their quest also as they journey to their next stop in ultimately reaching their destination

When I was growing up my parents planted certain mindsets in us as children. They would tell us that when we do things, make sure we do them well, but hearing that did not plant the importance or solidness of excellence and of being efficient at all. It sent the message do it right, so you won't have to do it over again, but it did not say beyond that.

As I grew older, going to school, completing certain levels of education, even then, the real effect, strength and power of these words did not really hit my mind, until I entered the working world. These words came up so often that I immediately had to make changes to ensure that during my assessments, I could be rewarded.

Then I started to grasp, accept and embrace the impact of this word, how powerful it is and when it is allowed to become part of my life in all areas the kind of results I can achieve and be very excited and happy with.

In closing this segment on the advantage, it must be very clear that you become fully aware of how important it is to ensure that as you work well with the advantage, you must begin to have some if not all of these great extraordinary experiences working in your life that will eventually make you a force to be reckoned with.

It will also allow you to live a phenomenal life that others can begin to emulate some area or areas and decide that is the life that they want to have and live and how you really want to be so involved in the system that gives you life beyond your wildest dreams and imagination.

Here they are:

1. **You be-come a great nation.** This does not mean that you must have lots of children to become a great nation but as you work with your family there are certain qualities and characteristics that denotes nationhood. Generally, most people begin to think about creed, class, rank, stock and birth, but this goes beyond these.

   Governments are designed to really make a nation out of its people amidst class color, creed, rank, stock or barrel. However, many governments have failed in seeing this God vision and becoming willing to make it happen. There are some governments that are striving to accomplish such. This should be the real idea of a flowing, effective and visionary government where it leads its people into becoming one nation to show their greatness, power, abilities and capabilities no matter whether the country is small or large.

Such characteristics and qualities are subjected to behaviors, personal operations, dreams, goals, oneness, unity and striving to achieve the common goal while at the same time empowering others to achieve theirs.

2. **Being blessed with abundant favors:** because of who you are and the behaviors exhibit, people will gladly assist you and go out of their way to be a big blessing to you. They will give to you, not from the point of exchange but because they just want to do something for you.

   People generally say favor is not fair, but it is essential to have favor working for you even when you are sleeping so that while you are awake you can breathe and relax at the outcome of favor being at work for you.

   Therefore, there is a reality about you that must be embraced and put to work: there is really no shortage in my life, no matter what is happening outside and around me. Abundant favors give me all the opportunities, and all the assistance and help I need.

3. **Your name becoming famous and distinguished:** Have you ever imagined or had deep thought and study of you becoming very famous and distinguished? Have you ever thought about what it would be like that wherever you show up and people realize it is you they just smile at you give you the thumbs up, or even request your autograph? There is this great buzz about you and you have become a household name? What excitement and atmosphere accompany such levels of living and being that you begin to converse with yourself and tell yourself, how good it feels, and you couldn't imagine it would be this welcoming and enjoyable.

   Well, it's time to use your imagination to such a level that it would allow you to embrace without reservation and accept this as your own reality and consciousness about your new life and start working towards making this happen.

4. **Being able to dispense good to others:** No matter what you may think or how you may feel about having lots of money and about people who do, there is a reality that all of us have to embrace: in order to be able to dispense good to others we must be possessors of what is good that we can increase and multiply it and then dispense it to others.

   Good come in many forms and very often the good that many people need right now is in the financial area. Others may need encouragement, impartation of wisdom and knowledge that they can use to assist them in going to the next level, but the bottom line is we must possess whatever is needed and have the mind and freedom that we can easily and willingly dispense it wherever it is needed.

   It's a law principle that however we use it, it will multiply in form, quality and value and come back to us. The time to possess what is needed for others is now so that we can keep this cycle moving and moving at the speed required by others.

5. **Those who confer blessings and Prosperity on you, God will bless.** This is so amazing and mind provoking. Very often we are of the mindset, that only those who do us evil we must assist to show how locked in we are in the Christian faith. However, God made it abundantly plain in the life of Abraham this is what will happen to those who act like me where you are concerned.

   It does not matter Abraham how much you have, in terms of wealth, the people who confer, who consult together about honoring, changing your life to a greater good or degree, those who are constantly thinking of ways to make you the father of many nations, the icon of your time, I will in turn ensure that they get to live and enjoy the life that you have and live

They must consult amongst themselves concerning the life that God has designed for you to live and then make plans to get involved in seeing and making that happen to you.

6. **Those who curse and oppose you, God will curse and oppose:** Then we realize that this is the very opposite to number 5 in the above. Those who have no reason to dislike you, plan your demise and destruction, God will take care of them.

    Very often we are overly concerned with how people are with us, how they sneak around behind our backs to disrespect, dishonor and shame us, threaten who we are, and what we have, that we can become distracted and lose our focus for the next level. But the set up here by God our heavenly Father is so extraordinary that while we push ahead He takes care of all that is going on publicly and in secret. What others might plan against us. It's time to fully trust God et up system.

    Always remember the great one is looking out on our behalf for us and will right the wrong where ourselves and others are concerned.

7. **In thee shall all families of the earth be blessed:** As I started to highlight in number 4, The mind must become so renewed and changed that everyone begins to accept the fact and reality that they need prosperity to make it for their families and then for others.

    The time is here for greater personal internal change, where the message of prosperity is concerned. You can never be a good blessing to others if there is lack and the struggle. Too long people have struggled so much and then they associate the struggle life to Christianity and holiness. **This mindset and belief are lies concerning the design of God andbto spell mistrust and send the message of doubt.**

The more people struggle as a nation it sends the message, the keepers and administrators of that nation are not doing their jobs or a good job as to what is required of them. People usually go to the polls to elect people they believe will manage and become creative to make policies to assist them in changing their lives to upgrade, enhance and rebrand their way of living.

As this is the expectation in the natural, then what about God our Heavenly Father who is the greatest and most Lovable Father. With God there is nothing called lack, struggle, or failure.

Therefore, the reality is here to understand that we are designed on the earth to live for each other and to be a blessing. They are people who need just words of encouragement, words to commend them to make them feel happy and to let them know they are doing a good job in what they are doing. The most shocking reality that many pretend they don't know is, there is a huge number of people who need some financial assistance and in a huge way to change their living conditions and to bring them up to more than just the basic way of living.

Based on how nations, countries, technology, even the weather has changed and is still changing; as we upgrade our country in areas of Proper scrutiny and election of high moral governments, technology, buildings, status, defense and Protection, Judiciary systems and the list goes on, it is unfair not to upgrade our people at every area of life. Hence the call is here for us to become possessors of abundant prosperity so that families can be blessed. This is what you and I should be doing until every family on the earth experiences a better life.

Now is the time to really decide what type of person you want to become and the kind of mark you want to impact life with and begin to pursue such as seriously and quickly as possible. Decide now how important it is to Take The Quantum Leap.

Finally, Unstoppable people make things go their way. They never compromise or accept anything other than the best; they know what they deserve because of how they have worked on themselves, and they continue to work on themselves to produce greater and higher versions of themselves.

They understand the importance of being relevant and on course for all times, they don't race or compete with time, they charge time to work with them and for them.

CHAPTER 8

Seeing the Future, Building and Creating Opportunities.

*N*ot all opportunities are open and clear before the eye, there are some that are very invisible and are waiting to be seen from that realm, or created and brought into the visible realm, our realm and existence.

With all this in mind not everyone can see just the future but I'm talking from the understanding of seeing a future but one that creates the opportunities, life changers, advancement, the ease at all levels and areas, the powers present and available to propel its people away from certain mindsets of struggle, failure, regret, sickness, death, Poverty, and the list goes on.

Based how on well and conscious you are of this visibility, then chances are you will become an impactful, life changing and timely creator.

Take note that whatever or whoever has been created can recreate and to recreate at a greater and more superior dimension of quality and quantity.

To create you should have an image of something that you can begin to use your **internal inherent** knowledge and powers to manipulate the details, concepts and finally produce the outcome of that thing that you envision.

Many organizations have remained alive, relevant and impactful because they understand how to rebrand, expand and create opportunities and in many cases how to change their concepts to be more meaningful and impactful.

They know the image they want to portray to the public, they have studied the public, what it would take to capture their attention and they make plans to be certain they have the public's attention and if not all the majority of it.

For many organizations, the idea of budgeting millions of dollars into feasibility studies in all areas of markets is very well welcomed, vital and pursued, however many individuals cannot afford the money and in many cases the time frame to do such. But in their own confines they can create and do their own studies with the markets and with that roving eye can visualize and envision the direction, markets or rather the world, the demand and people are going and begin to tailor their creative minds in the direction to produce opportunities.

Creating opportunities in the eyes of many may not be easy but when the premises of constantly soaring to new dimensions and heights are actively in place to achieve and present ways to experience different magnitudes of life, then it is clear the people / nation must properly be informed in a timely manner so they can maximize such opportunities and at the same time preparing themselves for such.

This is all about making the choice for your nation to experience all that everyone who desires such can achieve throughout their lifetime.

Before I continue, this must be clear in the mind and readily accepted, **"the creators of provision for our generation and others to come must have this mindset.** Things must not be so chaotic and because of what is happening a race with time and achievement becomes the norm. **We should never race with or misuse time, we envelop time and seek to have a clear understanding of how to function with time by knowing its rhythm, how to be in harmony with it, the sound it gives and what will attract it, to ensure that the picture we have of time is very clear and precise so that we can begin to work together with time, creating oneness and so that time works for and with us. There is no dispute or illusion where time is concerned."**

Wow, what do I mean by all that: have you ever had days when you got up and mentioned how you were in a flow and everything you planned to do just got done with more than enough time to spare?

Even on the job, **it appeared as though that day was designed from heaven**, people behaved differently, things worked so efficiently, you wanted to sing all through the office and if it was permitted, you could dance on your desk with joy? Your colleagues and you were so elated at how the day unfolded and all that took place, they even voiced their thoughts on how they wished every day was like that day?

Well, every day has been sent from heaven, heaven is on the job allowing us to have each day. The problem comes when people are out of the rhythm and flow with themselves and time.

The atmosphere they brought with them might not appropriate for great production, the ease or being able to produce new ideas to handle any challenge that might arise.

Whenever the environment is hostile there will always be a fight first, to think properly, then to act. In many cases where there is a huge amount of hostility that may not be personally directed but as long as it is present it will produce problems, and time has no choice but to sail along quickly to end that day. Time makes a very critical and conscious decision before things get more out of hand right here, right now, time decides let me use this huge hostility to let it appear as though time has run a race with lightning speed. So, when we catch ourselves, look at the clock, we say oh my, can't believe all that time has gone.

Therefore, based on the future we can see, we will be driven to create the opportunities that will support the future to make it brighter, greater and exciting. Remember the future is just one thought away.

There are many opinions about the future and sometimes it is not realized that the future will contain huge amounts of different ideas to contribute to its happenings and existence which in many cases do not suggest that many are right or wrong. However, we must be able to take a careful look at our present and then decide how and what we want the future to be like and make plans to contribute carefully to that area.

Currently, based on what is happening in our nation and around the world, there is the feeling and hesitation of expecting a great future. However, we must begin to believe that we can make a tremendous difference to assist in steering our nation in the direction it needs to go and to arrive there.

Recently, I have been carefully examining the way things are and train myself to have not just the idea or perception from my point of view but to look and examine with a greater eye what kind of future I would love to see and how it could impact the current generation and the others to come.

I realize, not only must there be the concentration of being financially stable and ensuring there is more than enough, **(money is very vital and necessary for proper survival and impact) but** putting great emphasis on reminding our people about having great values, high standards and the type of image they must be so careful in exhibiting. All of these helps to build a solid and profound structure for living, for impact and ensuring there is truly astounding longevity of a great legacy.

Besides those, there are certain foundational structures and systems that were implemented years ago, and have worked successfully then, but for today, there is a pressing need to redefine, upgrade and in many cases, rebrand to produce the greatest level of quality in building the future.

Even though those systems work very well for example **Dr. Martin Luther King had a dream** where one day the height and acceptance of segregation among people by the color of their skins, possession and status would become a thing of the past and one day there would be equality and every person, no matter, creed, culture, skin tone or national status would be given the same opportunity to prove themselves.

This dream was not supposed to be just that (where black and white would sit together whether in a bus or train, front or back) and go no further, that was not the full essence or magnitude of his dream. To make the dream relevant and produce what was not heard or not penned means that the right kind of people with the correct mindset would have to take time to study **this dream** to find the hidden mysteries and then be able to find the people who would be interested in making those mysteries known and seeing them become a reality.

Obviously, there will always be those who would discount its magnitude, and in many cases, try their utmost best to mis-interpret the magnitude of the dream to their own advantage and at the same time make it work to the disadvantage of many.

No matter what, this dream moved in power unknown and invisibly with unconscious aid and support, until America Had its First Black President.

I remembered, years ago when I was working, I attended lunch with my boss (at that time the president of a well-known oil company) and the employees, a mixture of black and white.

I was at the table with the president and some of my white colleagues and he (the boss) asked the question about President Obama (who was now running for the first time) whether He stood a chance in being elected president of America. One of my white colleagues promptly replied: "**Oh no, America is not ready for that level of change**" and I said to him in the presence of everyone, *"You and many might not be ready for such, but the age demands it, He (Mr. Obama) is going to be elected as President."*

Funny enough, the lady at that time who was senior to me behaved as though I didn't have a clue about what was happening in the world and more so in America. But it happened He was elected and not for one term but two successful terms and is now deemed as the most popular President of America.

One of the greatest lessons I learnt from the meeting and what actually happened in America, is that people can only relate from where they are, how they feel about certain people and things, also who they connect with but that does not mean that that they understand time or that they are on course with the world or the age.

Time and Age have listened and are still listening to certain dreams from the Divine realm that must be manifested, and they are staying on course to ensure when the fullness of time (when the time is fully ripe) comes what those divine powers have been asking and calling for, they must present it.

I must have laser vision, not just be short sighted or seeing only the now.

Even though he (President Obama) has finished his time, there is still the great and phenomenal buzz concerning him, his life and family. People and not just ordinary people, but all types and kinds of people want to keep track of him and his next move.

This all commenced through the dream that Dr. King had and look how the age took shape and made the dream spin into something that I'm sure many did not see coming or happening and on his first elected time it is said that more whites than blacks voted him in.

Very often it takes someone to see the future that is really needed and very often what they are bringing and saying very often does not sit well with people who are just seeing the present and have their selfish ideas about life. They only want things to work for them to make them greater and it gives them more destructive power.

You must be able to see the future that's relevant for the upcoming age, to properly contribute in building what is needed and building it right so that each generation when it's their time, understands their purpose and mandate in taking the lead, how to put their hands on the wheels to steer, whether it's a country and its people or a business as the age and time is expecting and waiting their arrival.

Therefore, it is going to take the right people to step forward and give their people new and lasting concepts that communicates that what they are building and want to continue to build will be part of the future because we can see the future that is really needed.

The idea of branding people and creating more barriers and destructive systems must be very quickly eradicated, (those outdated selfish, self-survival behaviors which only lead to hate) lest they continue to produce a future filled with all the unwanted and unnecessary trouble that puts any nation and its people in a frame of mind of total unrest, fear and unwanted expectancy.

When we have these adverse levels magnified it is going to lead to more riots, innocent deaths, hopes and dreams destroyed and the acceptance of living on the edge and becoming more chaotic at every level and dimension.

As it is right now, we have too many people who are in their own world and ideology and based on their operations and behaviors, if continued, will add major fear and fear in its working maturity will produce torment.

Time to build a future filled with all the attributes that denote nationhood, total security, equality, justice, truth, righteousness, compassion, acceptance, hope, happiness, love, joy and a peace that will lead to more ease and tranquility.

A future that will offer new and innovative ideas and concepts creating new opportunities for everyone to enhance their minds, time and perceptions for greater living and existence.

The urgent need for opportunities at every level is so strong and demanding in every nation. Many companies are now at the place where job cutbacks and the livelihood of people is threatened. The cutting back has become the norm and as time goes by it will become worse and there is no telling the magnitude and level that this will achieve.

With this trend we have to start re-visiting what we are doing and causing with a careful eye, mind and heart and ask ourselves the question whether we understand the world that we will be presenting to our kids and whether our kids are thoroughly equipped both mentally, physically and educationally to live well, do well and be well. I am very sure they will survive very long.

Therefore, it is imperative for those who will take the wheels to commence the future and drive it forward, to start releasing all personal ills and conflicts, which will allow them to see the bigger picture and what is required to actually make it happen.

The need to truly unite with the right people who will produce the correct thinking power, tools, strategies, abilities and the will and atmosphere is very necessary to the opening of new phenomenal opportunities.

There is a very loud and urgent cry (call, demand) for the uplifting of correct values, standards and protocol is needed to be at the forefront and to be displayed at all levels of operation. For this level of change to arrive quickly and urgently **I charge and ask the We all decide it's time to Take The Quantum Leap.**

Money and wealth and creed and status, these are also needed to take society to the next level, but we must ensure that the emphasis on standards, values and protocol is also understood, demanded and at the same level of these other criteria.

Urgently, it must be realized the need to commence teaching and re-chartering the course of values and to instill and implant them in our current and future generation, showing them, the type of consciousness and mindset required to move things forward in love, respect, honor harmony, mercy, compassion and unity.

Greater emphasis must be placed on values, (Personal, Corporate and Spiritual) which involves the need for correct discipline from a personal level which will be relevant for all levels and types of operations that will produce the highest quality of behaviors. With such great and tremendous heights of advancement, all areas of advancement must be taken very seriously.

Finally, **Taking the Quantum Leap is a choice everyone must be ready for and strive to assist others in taking theirs.** Whenever this leap is taken life can and will never be the same, the level of excitement grandeur and unbelievable experiences will create more open doors of opportunity filled with all the necessary tools, wisdom, knowledge and people you need to meet to have your ready, set, ordained and predestined encounters.

Don't be prepared to live life as usual or normal. The whole idea is to set your goals as high as you can and make the necessary preparations to start working with them to bring them into reality in this realm by Taking The Quantum Leap.